EVERYTHING YOU NEED TO KNOW BEFORE YOU'RE 18

(But Won't Get Taught in School)

100+ Essential Life Skills for Self-Confidence, Happiness, and Success

FERNE BOWE

Copyright © 2025 Ferne Bowe

Published by: Bemberton Ltd

All rights reserved. No part of this book or any portion thereof may be reproduced in any form by any electronic or mechanical means, without permission in writing from the publisher, except for the use of brief quotes in a book review.

The publisher accepts no legal responsibility for any action taken by the reader, including but not limited to financial losses or damages, both directly or indirectly incurred as a result of the content in this book.

ISBN: 978-1-915833-58-7

Disclaimer: The information in this book is general and designed to be for information only. While every effort has been made to ensure it is wholly accurate and complete, it is for general information only. It is not intended, nor should it be taken as professional advice. The author gives no warranties or undertakings whatsoever concerning the content. For matters of a medical nature, the reader should consult a doctor or other health care professional for specific health-related advice. The reader accepts that the author is not responsible for any action, including but not limited to losses both directly or indirectly incurred by the reader as a result of the content in this book.

View all our books at **bemberton.com**

CONTENTS

5	Introduction
7	Defining Success in Your Own Terms
23	Building Resilience for Life's Challenges
37	Exploring Your Post-School Options
51	Launching Your Career: Navigating Opportunities and Growth
67	Building Your Own Space: Navigating Housing, Roommates, and Transportation
83	Building Financial Strength: Managing Money for Your Future
107	Mastering Digital Tools for Your Life: Staying Safe and Smart Online
123	Prioritizing Your Health: Building a Strong Foundation
131	Building Healthy Eating Habits: Fueling Your Body for Success
143	Building Your Support System: Cultivating Strong and Healthy Relationships
165	Conclusion

BEMBERTON
BOOKS

SOMETHING FOR YOU

Thanks for buying this book. To show our appreciation, here's a **FREE** printable copy of the "Life Skills for Tweens Workbook"

WITH OVER 80 FUN ACTIVITIES JUST FOR TWEENS!

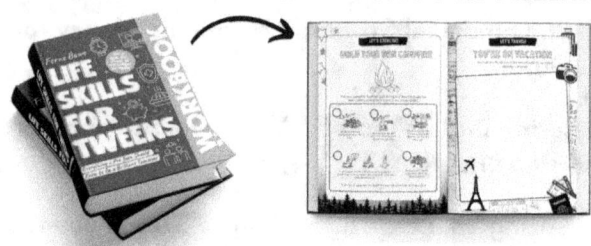

Scan the code to download your FREE printable copy

INTRODUCTION

Welcome to one of life's biggest adventures — becoming an adult! Whether you're heading to college, starting work, or figuring out your next move, you're standing at the edge of something incredible. It's exciting, maybe a little scary, and absolutely packed with possibilities.

Did you know that at 18, you can vote, sign contracts, and even start your own business? These are major powers that come with serious responsibilities. The thing is, most of us are handed these "adulting" roles without anyone teaching us the essential skills we need to handle them. When was the last time you learned how to build credit, budget for an apartment, or tackle a tough conversation at work?

Your late teens and early 20s are full of "firsts" — first job interviews, first apartments, and first serious relationships. These experiences shape who you'll become. While you'll definitely make some mistakes along the way (we all do!), each experience is a chance to learn and grow stronger.

That's where this book comes in. Think of it as your personal guide to mastering the life skills that school probably didn't teach you. Inside, you'll discover how to:

- **Build your independence (master finances, housing, career)**
- **Take care of yourself (health, well-being, safety)**
- **Make smart decisions (planning, responsibilities)**
- **Create strong connections (relationships, networking, community)**

This isn't a boring textbook — it's more like having a conversation with someone who's been there. Each chapter tackles a different subject in depth, and is packed with practical advice and real-world guidance that you can use right away.

How to use this book:
- Read chapters in order, or jump to what you need.
- Try the exercises and self-assessments.
- Use the checklists and worksheets to track your progress.
- Keep notes on what resonates with you.
- Return to sections as new challenges arise.

Remember, everyone's path is different, and that's 100% okay. Take what works for you, adapt it to your situation, and know that stumbling sometimes is just part of the journey. This is your time to explore, grow, and build the foundation for the life you want to create.

Let's get started!

DEFINING SUCCESS IN YOUR OWN TERMS

"Success is not about how much money you make; it's about the difference you make in people's lives."
— Michelle Obama

When you think of success, what comes to mind? Maybe you picture a powerful businessperson making big decisions or a world-famous artist performing for adoring fans. Perhaps you imagine a happy grandparent surrounded by family, or something else entirely. Success can look different for everyone, and that's okay. The key is to understand what success means to you, rather than letting someone else define it for you.

Before we dive deeper into understanding success, take a moment to reflect:

- What does success look like to you right now?
- What would make you feel proud in 5 years?
- What's holding you back from achieving your goals?
- What support do you need to move forward?

Your answers might change as you read this chapter, and that's perfectly normal.

What Really Defines Success?

We often see wealth and social status as markers of success, but many people who have these things still don't find fulfillment. While money and fame can be a part of success, they are not the core of it. True success typically encompasses several key elements:

- **Freedom of Choice:** Having the autonomy to make decisions that align with your values
- **Personal Satisfaction:** The joy and fulfillment that come from pursuing what genuinely matters to you

Meaningful Contributions: Making a positive impact on the world, however big or small

Success Myths vs. Reality:

Common Myths:
- Success means being rich.
- Success requires sacrificing everything else.
- Success happens overnight.
- There's only one path to success.

Reality:
- Success looks different for everyone.
- Balance is crucial for lasting success.
- Success is a journey of small wins.
- There are many paths to achieve your goals.

By focusing on these core elements, you can define success in a way that aligns with your values. Chasing external validation, like wealth or fame, rarely leads to lasting happiness. There's always more to earn and more attention to seek, but, like running on a treadmill, you end up feeling stuck. This endless chase can lead to stress and dissatisfaction, no matter how "successful" you appear to others.

Discovering Your Own Path to Success

> *"Success is liking yourself, liking what you do,
> and liking how you do it."*
> **— Maya Angelou**

Everyone's vision of success is unique. For some, it might mean climbing the corporate ladder, while for others it could mean making art, raising a family, or finding the perfect work-life balance. Everyone's version of success is different, and that's what makes it personal and meaningful. Instead of basing your choices on what others define as success, think about what it means for you.

> **Real-Life Success Stories:**
> - **Sarah, 19:** Defined success as starting her own small online business while studying.
> - **Marcus, 18:** Found success in balancing sports training with academic achievement.
> - **Jenna, 20:** Measured success by her ability to help others through volunteer work.
>
> These stories show us that success isn't one-size-fits-all. Each person found fulfillment in a different way that aligned with their values and goals.

Let's reflect on your definition of success with these questions:
- What activities and interests bring you joy?
- What values are most important to you?
- How do you want to impact your community and the world?
- What kind of legacy do you want to leave?

Your answers can help form your "personal success statement" — this isn't set in stone; it can evolve as you grow and learn more about yourself.

> **The Success Formula:**
> **Preparation + Opportunity + Action**
>
> While luck plays a role, success usually follows this pattern:
> - **Preparation:** Building skills and knowledge
> - **Opportunity:** Recognizing and finding chances to use your preparation
> - **Action:** Taking decisive steps when opportunities arise
>
> Example: Landing Your First Job
> - Preparation: Creating a strong resume, practicing interview skills
> - Opportunity: Finding suitable job openings
> - Action: Applying and following through with strong interviews

The Role of Luck, Hard Work, and Opportunity

"The harder I work, the luckier I get."
— Samuel Goldwyn

Success is rarely about pure luck or pure effort — it's usually a combination of the two. While you can't control luck, you can:

- Position yourself for opportunities.
- Develop skills that make you valuable.
- Build a network that connects you to possibilities.
- Stay ready to seize chances when they arise.

Success isn't about waiting for the perfect moment — it's about preparing for the moments that come your way.

What Is Luck, Really?

Luck is a tricky concept. Some people seem to have it all, while others feel like they have none. But often, those who feel "lucky" are simply more open to opportunities and have a positive mindset that attracts more possibilities. This doesn't mean ignoring reality — it means being ready to act when chances arise and turning challenges into stepping stones.

THE POWER OF POSITIVITY

How do you start to "feel lucky"? For some, it comes naturally, but for others, it takes effort. **The first step is to think positively.** A positive mindset helps you embrace opportunities, build resilience, and make the most of every situation. It's not about being happy all the time or having unrealistic expectations — it's about facing each day with openness and understanding that you get out of situations what you put into them.

Here are some ways to develop a positive mindset:

- **Look after yourself:** Your mental and physical health are the foundation of a positive mindset. Prioritize healthy eating, sleep, exercise, and relaxation each day.
- **Practice gratitude:** Every day, take a few minutes to write down what you're thankful for.
- **Be compassionate:** Replace negative thoughts with compassionate ones.
- **Face challenges head-on:** View obstacles as learning opportunities. Instead of waiting for things to get better, take proactive steps to make them better.
- **Choose positive people:** The people you spend time with shape your outlook. Surround yourself with those who uplift and inspire you.
- **Celebrate small wins:** Recognize and celebrate your achievements, no matter how small.

- **Track your progress:** Keep a journal of your achievements, no matter how small.
- **Create a success routine:** Develop daily habits that move you toward your goals.
- **Find role models:** Study people who've achieved what you want to achieve.
- **Learn from setbacks:** Use challenges as learning opportunities.

FINDING AND CREATING YOUR OWN OPPORTUNITIES

"Fortune befriends the bold."
— Emily Dickinson

While some opportunities might find you, the most successful people actively create and pursue their opportunities. Think of it like fishing — you need to:

- Know where to fish (identify promising areas)
- Use the right bait (develop attractive skills)
- Be patient (persist through quiet periods)
- Be ready to act (recognize when to "reel in" an opportunity)

Being open to new experiences and challenges is key to spotting opportunities. Here are some ways to get started:

- **Know your strengths and interests:** Create a list of your skills, talents, and passions. Ask yourself:
    - What tasks do you excel at naturally?

- What activities make you lose track of time?
- What do others often compliment you on?
- What topics do you love learning about?

- **Stay informed:** Even after you've left school, commit to a life of learning:
  - Follow industry leaders on social media.
  - Subscribe to relevant newsletters.
  - Take online courses or workshops.
  - Listen to podcasts in your field.

- **Network and connect:** Meet new people and build meaningful connections:
  - Attend industry events and meetups.
  - Join online communities in your field.
  - Reach out to people you admire.
  - Offer help before asking for favors.
  - Follow up and maintain relationships.

- **Cultivate curiosity:** Approach new situations with enthusiasm:
  - Try new approaches to familiar tasks.
  - Volunteer for challenging projects.
  - Share your expertise and collaborate with others.
  - Welcome feedback and new perspectives.

Be Curious and Embrace a Growth Mindset

"I have not failed. I've just found 10,000 ways that don't work."
— ***Thomas Edison***

A growth mindset means believing that your abilities can be developed through dedication and hard work. It's the opposite of a fixed mindset, which sees talents as unchangeable traits. Here's how they differ:

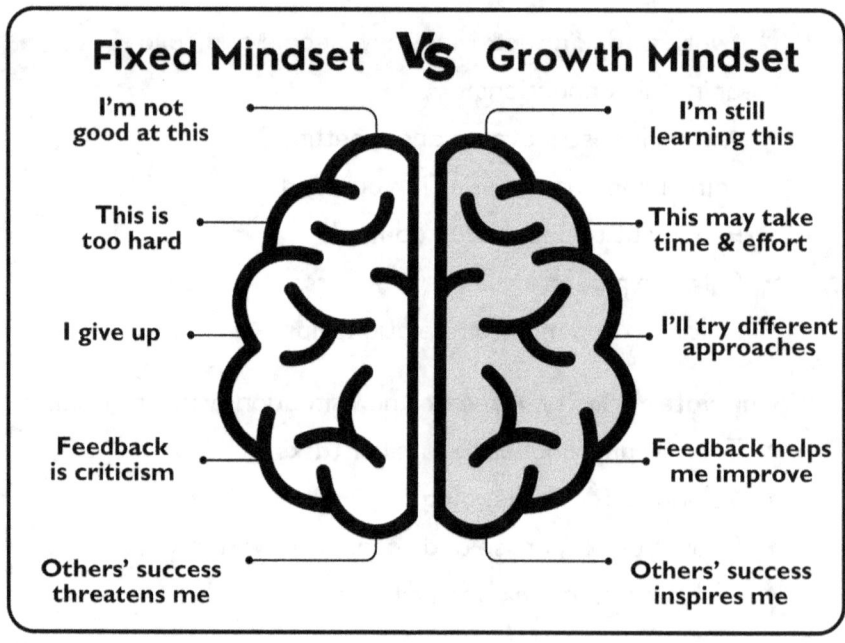

A growth mindset is about staying curious, being open-minded, and learning from mistakes. Here's how to cultivate it:

- **Stay curious and keep learning:** Life is an ongoing journey of change and learning:
  - Make time for learning new skills.
  - Explore new hobbies, interests, and paths that push you outside your comfort zone.
  - Ask questions and seek out learning and understanding.

- **Embrace challenges:** Try to view obstacles as growth opportunities:
  - Reframe mistakes and failures as learning opportunities.
  - Celebrate your effort and hardwork, not just outcomes.

- **Seek out feedback:** Use feedback from teachers, mentors, and peers to improve yourself:
  - Ask questions.
  - Try to listen without defensiveness.
  - Create action plans based on feedback.

- **Reframe negative thoughts:** Try to change your self-talk:
  - From: "I'm not good at this" → To: "I'm getting better at this."
  - From: "This is too hard" → To: "This will take practice."
  - From: "I made a mistake" → To: "I learned something new."

SLOW AND STEADY WINS THE RACE

It's tempting to want — or even expect — immediate results in all aspects of life. Unfortunately, that's just not how things work. Real results come from long-term effort. Give yourself time and commit to slow, incremental improvement.

Set Meaningful Goals

The next step toward building success is establishing effective goals. Goals are powerful tools that apply to every aspect of life and guide your journey. They provide clear targets to aim for and concrete ways to measure progress while remaining flexible enough to adapt as circumstances change. Setting meaningful goals transforms abstract aspirations into achievable outcomes and creates momentum toward your definition of success.

What Makes an Effective Goal?

Not all goals are created equal. They should ideally be both inspiring and actionable. An effective goal should:

- Inspire you to take action
- Connect to your personal values
- Push you beyond your comfort zone

- Break down into easily manageable steps
- Have a clear measure of success

SMART Goals

The SMART framework is a simple way to transform your dreams into achievable goals:

- Before SMART: "I want to save money."
- After SMART: "I will save $2,000 for an emergency fund by December 31st by depositing $200 per month from my part-time job."

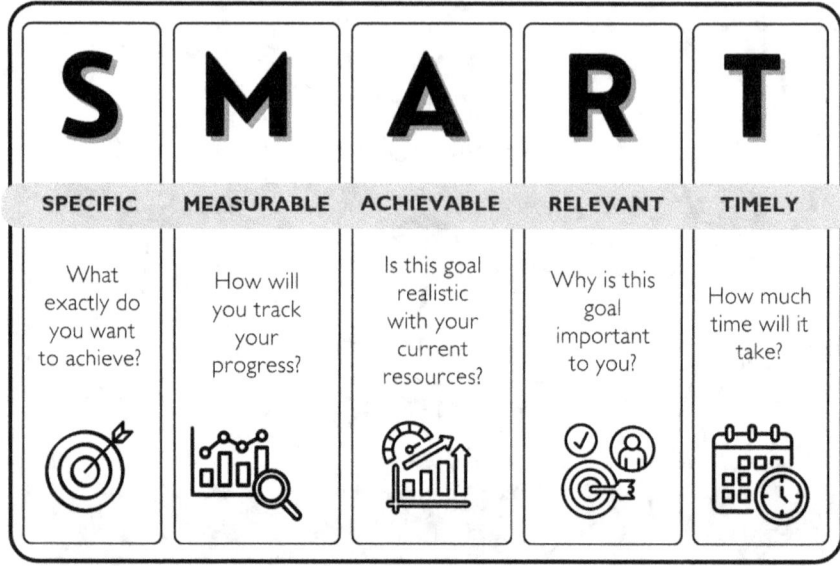

- **Specific:** What exactly do you want to achieve?
- **Measurable:** How will you know you're making progress?
- **Achievable:** Is this realistic with your current resources?
- **Relevant:** Does this matter to you and align with your larger goals?
- **Time-bound:** When exactly will you achieve this?

Set Your Own SMART Goal

Try setting your own SMART goal and outline the steps you'll take to achieve it.

1. Choose one area you want to improve.

2. Write your initial goal.

3. Apply the SMART criteria:
   - Specific: Clear and detailed
   - Measurable: Trackable progress
   - Achievable: Within your capabilities
   - Relevant: Aligns with your values
   - Time-bound: Has a deadline

4. Break it down into weekly actions.

5. Set up progress review points.

Here's how to transform a basic goal into a SMART goal.

Example: Basic goal: "I will raise my English grade from C to B by the end of this semester."

SMART example: "By June 15th (T), I will improve my English grade from C to B (S, M) by completing all assignments on time, attending twice-weekly study groups, and meeting with my teacher monthly for feedback (A). This aligns with my goal of studying journalism in college (R)."

Progress Check Points:
- Weekly: Review study habits and assignment grades.
- Monthly: Meet with teacher, adjust study strategies.
- Mid-term: Evaluate overall progress.
- End of semester: Final grade assessment and reflection.

Setting Up for Success

*"Success is stumbling from failure to failure
with no loss of enthusiasm."*
— Winston Churchill

By now, you probably realize that success isn't a final destination — it's an ongoing journey of growth, learning, and achievement.

Key Takeaways

- Success is personal and unique to you.
- Preparation + Opportunity + Action = Results.
- Your mindset shapes your outcomes.
- SMART goals turn dreams into plans.

Moving Forward

You now have the foundation for defining and pursuing your own vision of success, but life rarely follows a straight path — there will be obstacles, setbacks, and unexpected challenges along the way. That's why resilience is crucial.

The next chapter covers common challenges, strategies for dealing with setbacks, and tips for using these challenges to your advantage.

BUILDING RESILIENCE FOR LIFE'S CHALLENGES

"It is not the strongest of the species that survive, nor the most intelligent, but the one most responsive to change."
— **Charles Darwin**

Think about the last time you faced a significant challenge. How did you handle it? What helped you get through? What do you wish you'd done differently?

> ### Resilience Quiz
>
> Rate yourself from 1-5 on these statements:
>
> - ☐ I bounce back quickly from setbacks
> - ☐ I see challenges as opportunities
> - ☐ I maintain perspective during difficult times
> - ☐ I ask for help when needed
> - ☐ I learn from my mistakes
>
> Scoring
>
> **20-25:** Strong resilience foundation
> **15-19:** Growing resilience skills
> **Below 15:** Room for developing resilience strategies

The good news is that resilience — the ability to adapt, recover, and grow from adversity — is a skill you can develop. This chapter will help you build the tools to manage stress, anxiety, and the challenges that life will inevitably bring.

Understanding the Resilience Cycle

Resilience isn't something you're born with — it's something you build over time through experience and practice. Here's how it works:

1. **Challenge** → You face a difficult situation (failing a test, rejection, loss).

2. **Response** → Your initial reaction (stress, fear, anger — all normal).

3. **Adaptation** → You adjust and find new approaches (changing study habits, exploring alternatives).

4. **Growth** → You discover inner strength and develop new coping skills.

5. **Preparation** → You apply these lessons to future challenges, making you more resilient each time.

The key is that each cycle makes you stronger. Like building muscle, resilience grows with every challenge you overcome.

Understanding Stress and Anxiety

Stress and anxiety are your body's natural responses to challenging situations. While they can feel uncomfortable, understanding how they work helps you manage them better. Think of them as your body's alarm system — helpful when properly tuned, but problematic if too sensitive.

STRESS RESPONSE CYCLE

Stress is your body's response to a perceived threat. It usually follows a predictable cycle:

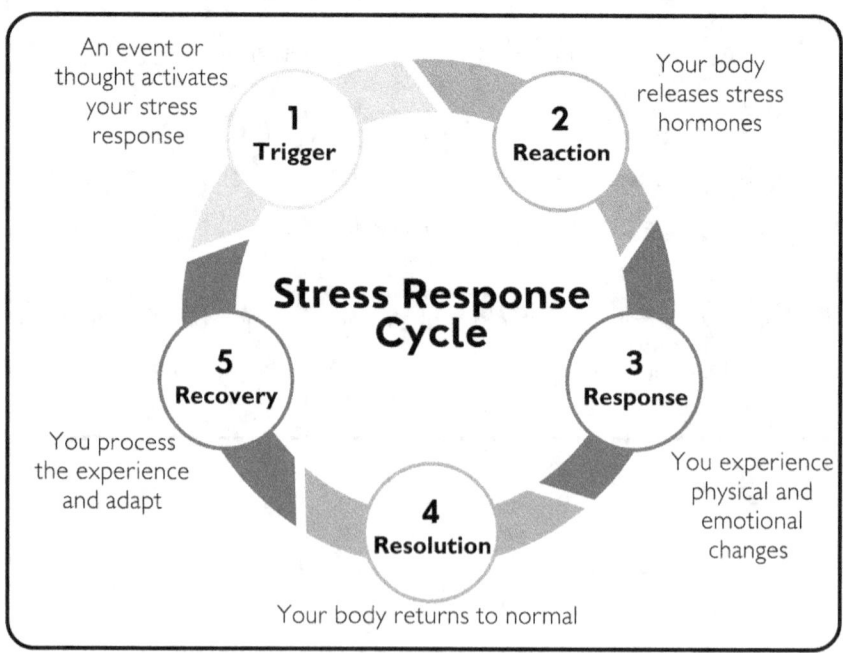

Understanding Your Stress Response

When you feel stressed, your body activates its "fight or flight" response. This happens whether you're:

- Facing a work deadline
- Taking an important test
- Having a difficult conversation
- Dealing with financial pressure
- Managing relationship challenges

While helpful in short bursts, this response can cause harm if constantly activated.

Prehistoric vs. Modern Stress

The stress response evolved when humans faced immediate physical threats—predators, rival groups, and environmental dangers. After escaping to safety, our ancestors could relax and end their stress response.

Modern stressors are different. They're often psychological and ongoing and not always easy to escape from. While the stress response remains effective for immediate threats, it's poorly suited to modern challenges like college applications or work deadlines. In these situations, the old-school stress responses don't help resolve the stressor.

> Quick Stress Assessment:
> - Which type of stress affects you most?
> - How does each type show up in your life?
> - What triggers your stress response?

TYPES OF STRESS

Understanding different types of stress helps you recognize and manage them better. Common types include:

- **Acute Stress:** The most common type of short-term response to specific situations. Examples include:
  - Preparing for an exam
  - Going on a first date
  - Playing in a sports match

- **Chronic Stress:** Ongoing, long-term stress that wears you down; the most harmful to physical and mental health. Sources include:
  - Family conflicts
  - School pressure
  - Health issues

- **Environmental Stress:** Stress caused by your surroundings:
  - Noisy environments
  - Crowded spaces
  - Poor lighting

- **Change-Related Stress:** Triggered by life changes:
  - Moving to a new place
  - Starting college/work
  - Relationship changes

- **Relationship Stress:** Tensions from challenging dynamics:
  - Friend conflicts
  - Dating challenges
  - Social pressures

THE EFFECTS OF STRESS ON THE BODY

Understanding how stress affects your body helps you recognize warning signs early. Think of it like your car's dashboard warnings — catching issues early prevents bigger problems.

Short-Term Signs
- Tense muscles
- Rapid heartbeat
- Shallow breathing
- Stomach issues
- Sleep problems
- Headaches

Long-Term Effects
- Weakened immune system
- Digestive problems
- Heart issues
- Sleep disorders
- Weight changes
- Chronic fatigue

UNDERSTANDING ANXIETY

While stress is your response to immediate challenges, anxiety is the persistent fear or anticipation of stressful situations. Types of anxiety include:

- **Situational:** Anxiety linked to specific events (tests, presentations)
- **Social:** Anxiety related to interactions with others
- **General:** Ongoing worries about various life issues
- **Performance:** Anxiety connected to achievements and meeting expectations

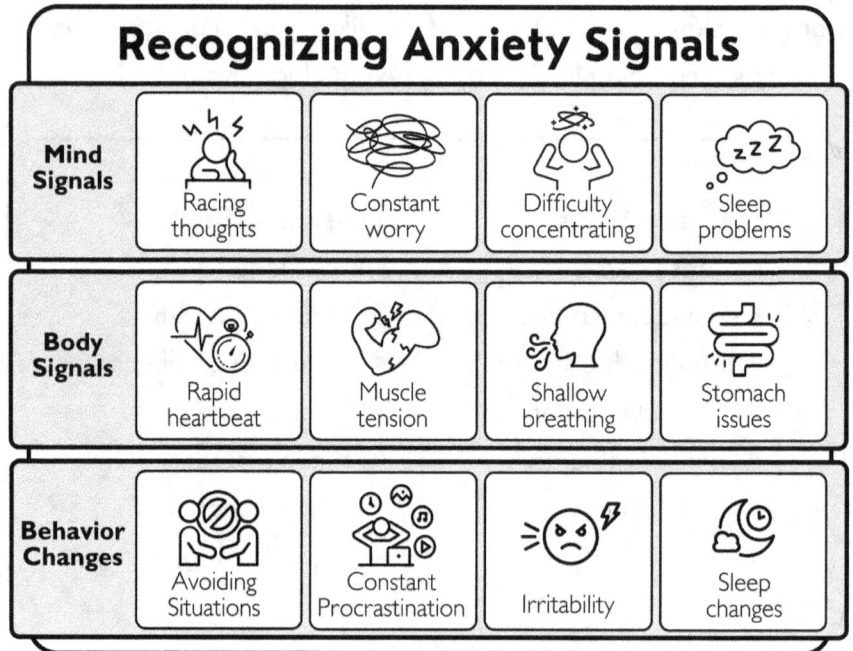

STRATEGIES TO DEAL WITH STRESS AND ANXIETY

Everyone faces stress and anxiety, so it's important to build a personal toolkit of coping strategies. Adopting these strategies now will help you manage stress throughout your life and protect your wellbeing.

The first step in dealing with stress is identifying what's causing it. Family, school, work, and friends, can all be sources of stress. Examine your life and the areas where the pressure builds up. What are your top sources of stress?

When stress hits, try these proven techniques (but seek professional help if feeling overwhelmed):

Immediate Relief Strategies:
- Deep breathing exercises (5 counts in, 7 counts out)
- Tense and relax each muscle group, moving from toes to head
- Take a quick walk or stretch
- Mindfulness exercises
- Grounding techniques

Long-Term Management:
- Exercise 3-4 times per week mixing cardio and strength training
- Maintain a consistent sleep schedule
- Eat regular meals with plenty of whole foods and vegetables
- Break large projects down into smaller chunks
- Build your network of friends through clubs, sports teams or support groups

Building Everyday Resilience

"Courage doesn't always roar. Sometimes, courage is the quiet voice at the end of the day saying 'I will try again tomorrow.'"
— **Mary Anne Radmacher**

Just like building physical strength requires regular exercise, building resilience requires daily practice. The good news is that every challenge you face is an opportunity to strengthen your resilience.

- **Quality Sleep:** Good sleep is your foundation for resilience. Aim for:
  - Consistent sleep/wake times
  - 8–10 hours per night
  - Screen-free time before bed
  - Comfortable sleep environment

- **Regular Movement:** Physical activity builds the body and mind:
  - Daily movement (even brief walks)
  - Exercise that you enjoy
  - Outdoor activities (when possible)
  - Stretch breaks during study/work

- **Nourishing Food:** What you eat affects how you feel:
  - Regular meals
  - Balanced healthy diet

- Stay hydrated
- Limited caffeine and sugary drinks

- **Mental Training:** Train your mind like you train your body:
  - Daily quiet time
  - Breathing exercises
  - Meditation practice

DEVELOPING POSITIVE COPING MECHANISMS

When stress hits, having healthy ways to cope makes all the difference. Think of these strategies as your personal emergency toolkit — ready when you need them.

- **Build your support network**: No one succeeds alone. Your support network might include:
  - Family members who understand you
  - Friends who lift you up
  - Teachers or mentors who guide you
  - Counselors or coaches who help you grow

- **Find your release valve**: Everyone needs healthy ways to release stress. Find what works for you:
  - Physical activity
  - Creative expression
  - Music or art
  - Time in nature
  - Hobbies you enjoy

- **Practice self-compassion**: Treat yourself with the same kindness you'd show a good friend:
  - Acknowledge your efforts
  - Accept that mistakes happen
  - Learn from setbacks
  - Celebrate small wins

- **Maintain perspective**: When problems feel overwhelming, step back and ask:
  - Will this matter in a year?
  - What can I learn from this?
  - What's still going well?
  - Who can help me with this?

Finding Support When You Need It

Everybody needs help sometimes — there's no shame in it. If you notice signs of overwhelm, like persistent fatigue, trouble concentrating, or feeling disconnected, it's important to seek support.

Know When to Reach Out

Watch for these signs that you might need extra support:
- Feeling overwhelmed for extended periods
- Changes in sleep or eating patterns
- Difficulty managing daily tasks
- Loss of interest in activities you usually enjoy
- Persistent feelings of anxiety or sadness

Where to Find Help

1. Talk to Those Close to You

Start with people you trust:
- Family members
- Close friends
- Teachers or counselors
- Sports coaches or activity leaders
- Religious or community leaders

2. Seek Professional Support

Professional help is available when you need it:
- School counselors
- Mental health professionals
- Support groups
- Youth services
- Online counseling services

3. Online and Phone Support

24/7 help is available through:
- Crisis helplines
- Text support services
- Online chat counseling
- Mental health apps
- Support forums

Remember: **Seeking support isn't a sign of weakness — it's a sign of wisdom and self-awareness**. Sometimes, the strongest thing you can do is ask for help.

Resilience for a Successful Life

Life brings challenges, but resilience helps transform them into opportunities for growth. This vital skill helps you recover quickly from difficulties, navigate unexpected changes effectively, extract valuable lessons from every challenge, develop greater emotional strength, and guide others through hard times.

Key Takeaways

- Stress and anxiety are normal parts of life.
- Resilience can be learned and strengthened.
- Everyone needs support sometimes.
- Small daily habits build long-term strength.
- It's okay to ask for help.

Moving Forward

Now that you understand how to build resilience and manage stress, you're better equipped to handle everyday challenges. This foundation will be especially valuable as you navigate important decisions about your future.

In the next chapter, we'll explore one of the biggest decisions you'll face: what to do after leaving school. Let's look at your options and how to choose the path that feels right for you.

EXPLORING YOUR POST-SCHOOL OPTIONS

*"You have brains in your head. You have feet in your shoes.
You can steer yourself any direction you choose."*
— **Dr. Seuss**

"What do you want to do after school?" It's a question that you've probably heard often. Deciding what to do after school can feel overwhelming, given the wide array of options available and the many opinions others share about your path. Remember though — this is your unique journey.

Before exploring your options, take time to consider:
- Which aspects of your future excite you most?
- What kind of lifestyle would fulfill you?
- What skills and strengths have you already developed?
- Which new abilities would you like to build?

Understanding Your Options

Leaving school opens a new chapter filled with possibilities. Whether you have a clear path in mind or are still exploring, understanding your choices is crucial. Here are some of the main options to consider:

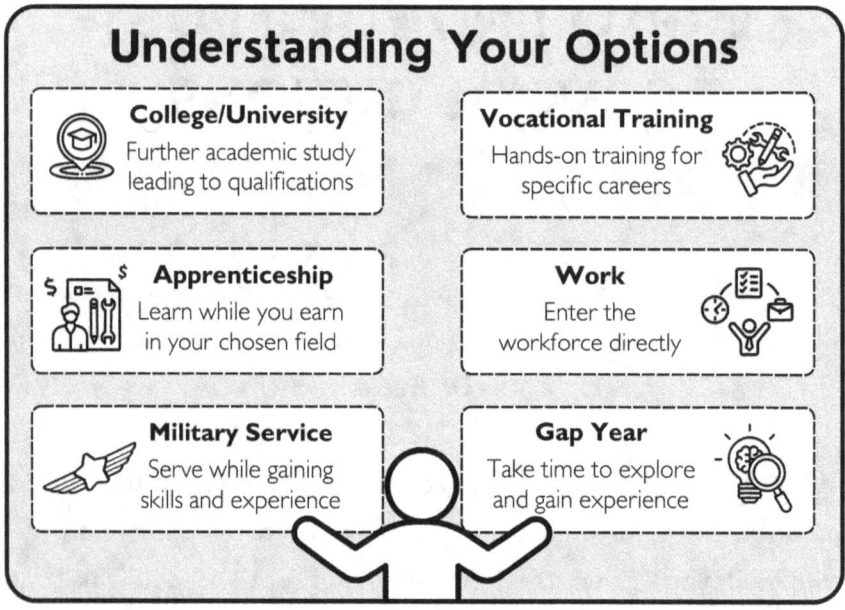

Each path offers unique benefits and challenges. The best choice for you depends on your interests and talents, financial situation, available opportunities, and personal circumstances. Remember, you can always change paths later, if needed. Choose what aligns best with your goals, not what others expect of you.

COLLEGE AND UNIVERSITY

Universities and colleges offer more than just degrees — they provide opportunities for:

- Deep learning in a chosen field
- Development of analytical thinking
- Career preparation
- Personal independence and growth

What to Consider:

- **Course Length:** Most degrees take three to four years.
- **Entry Requirements:** Specific grades or qualifications needed.
- **Study Style:** Lectures, seminars, independent research.
- **Costs:** Tuition, living expenses, study materials.
- **Location:** Local vs. moving away options.

VOCATIONAL TRAINING

Vocational training focuses on specific career skills through:
- Combined academic study with hands-on learning
- Industry-specific and/or professional qualifications
- Direct career pathways
- Work experience opportunities

Popular fields include:
- Health care services (e.g., nursing)
- Construction trades (e.g., carpentry)

- Cooking and culinary skills (e.g., working as a chef)
- Beauty and wellness (e.g., beauty therapy)
- Automotive technology (e.g., mechanics)

Apprenticeships

Apprenticeships offer the chance to earn while you learn, combining work experience, study, and a regular wage. While learning from experienced professionals, you'll gain:

- Hands-on experience in your chosen field
- Recognized qualifications
- Professional networks and connections
- Regular income while training

Popular areas include engineering, construction, digital technology, and hospitality, with new types of apprenticeships emerging as industries evolve.

Entering the Workforce

If you prefer to start earning immediately, entering the workforce after school could be the right choice. Starting work right away provides immediate income and real-world experience. Many successful careers begin in retail, hospitality, or office work — areas that offer room for growth and often support further training.

Key benefits include:
- Immediate income
- Real-world experience
- Potential for quick advancement
- On-the-job learning opportunities

MILITARY SERVICE

Military service provides a unique path combining career development, education, and personal growth. In addition to serving your country, you'll receive structured training, leadership opportunities, and valuable life experience.

GAP YEAR

A gap year provides time to reflect, travel, or volunteer before diving back into education or work. This isn't about taking a year off — it's about taking a year on to explore, learn, and grow in different ways. Many people use this time to:

- Travel and experience different cultures
- Volunteer for causes they care about
- Work and save money
- Learn new skills
- Figure out their next steps

Do It Yourself

If you want to develop your skills and knowledge without formal education, there's a wealth of online resources available. You can learn about almost any topic — from coding to philosophy — at your own pace. Platforms like Coursera, Khan Academy, and FutureLearn provide respected courses, many of which are free. Even tech giants like Google offer professional certifications that can lead to real career opportunities.

Finding the Right Path: Should College Be Your First Step?

College or university is a great option for those who want to study academic subjects or need a degree for their chosen career, but it's not the only path. Consider what aligns with your interests and future goals. Do you have a specific career in mind, or are you more interested in a certain lifestyle or type of work? Make decisions based on your goals, not external expectations.

Remember, this is just a starting point for thinking about your options. There's no wrong choice, and you can always change direction later.

Quick Quiz: Find Your Path

If you're unsure about your next steps after school, that's normal. This simple quiz can help guide you. Write down your answers to each question and check your result at the end.

1. Which of the following interests you most?
  A. Formal academic study (e.g., math, sciences, history)
  B. Hands-on activities (e.g., fixing, making, understanding how things work)
  C. Traveling, volunteering, and new experiences

2. What are your thoughts on continuing formal education?
  A. Excited to earn a degree
  B. Prefer practical skills with some study
  C. Need a break from formal study, but might return later

Your Results
If you chose mostly:
A's — Consider exploring university or college options.
B's — Look into vocational training or apprenticeships.
C's — Think about taking some time out to explore your interests.

Making Your Choice

Deciding whether to attend college or pursue another path is a significant decision. Take your time, consider the pros and cons of each option, and keep your goals and values in mind. Seek advice from friends, family and other trusted sources, but don't feel obligated to follow it.

College or university is often presented as the "best" option, but this isn't true for everyone. While academic study suits some, learning a trade or gaining work experience can be more interesting and lucrative for others. Given the cost of university, it's essential to ensure it aligns with your goals before committing.

Remember, your future is flexible. If you decide a degree isn't right for you now, you can always pursue one later. And if you're uncertain about what to do next, taking some time out to think is a great choice.

Lifelong Learning

No matter which path you choose, learning doesn't stop when school ends. The world is constantly changing, and staying adaptable means continually developing new skills and knowledge. You'll need a mix of:

- **Soft Skills:** Critical thinking, problem-solving, communication, and collaboration

- **Hard Skills:** Technical abilities specific to your chosen field
- **Adaptability:** Being ready to learn new things as technology and industries evolve

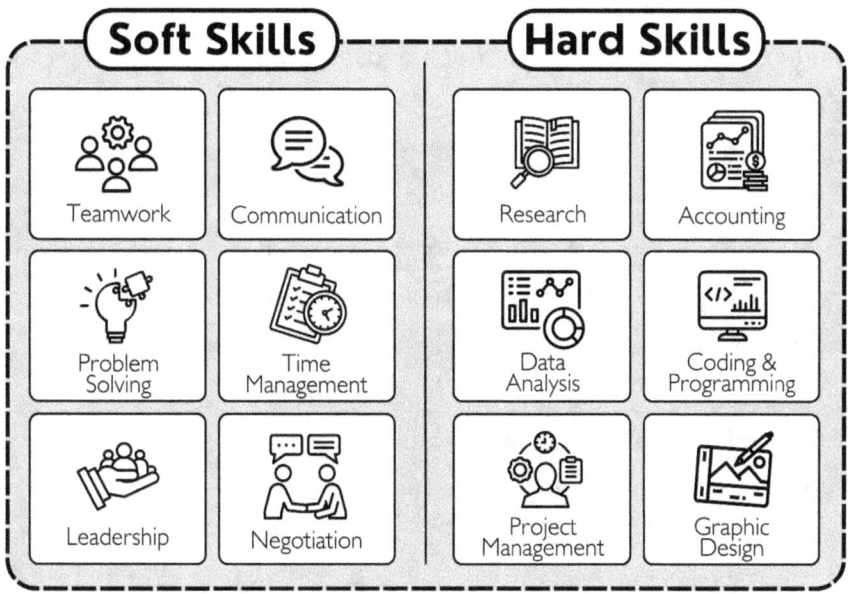

Navigating Your College or University Application

If you decide college is the right path for you, you'll need to navigate the application process. Application systems differ globally, so check with your school or college to find out the necessary steps and deadlines. Remember, higher education institutions vary in style, culture, and specialties, so it is important to research not only the course, but also the institution itself.

Beyond the Classroom: Making the Most of Your Experience

College (or any other new experience) isn't just about classroom learning — it's also a time to develop social skills, make connections, and explore new interests. The friendships and skills you cultivate during this time will last a lifetime, so make the most of your time and enjoy it!

Say "yes" to opportunities that come your way. Join research projects, pursue internships, join clubs, play sports, or volunteer to meet new people and build a well-rounded experience.

Take a minute to think about:
- What will you say "yes" to?
- What kind of experiences do you want to try that can help you grow both personally and professionally?

Being on Your Own

Heading off to college or university is often the first time many students live away from home. Moving away from family and friends can bring up feelings of loneliness and uncertainty, and that's completely normal. The good news? You're not alone in feeling this way. The key is not letting these emotions take over. Here's how you can cope and thrive:

- **Remember Resilience**: Every challenge you face helps build resilience. Be patient with yourself as you adjust. Celebrate small wins, whether making a new friend or finding your favorite study spot. You've got this.
- **Have Realistic Expectations**: It's okay if it takes time to settle in. Everyone's experience is different. Resist comparing yourself to others — they may be feeling just as unsure as you, even if they look like they've got it all figured out.
- **Build a Support Network**: Don't hesitate to reach out. Your professors, campus staff, and fellow students are there to help. If someone invites you to an event or activity, say yes! It might feel intimidating at first, but making new connections is the key to finding your place.
- **Look After Yourself**: Eating well, getting enough sleep, and staying active can work wonders for your mental health. Make time for activities you enjoy, and be mindful of avoiding unhealthy habits like excessive drinking or stress eating.
- **Seek Help When Needed**: If you're feeling overwhelmed, consider reaching out to on-campus counseling services or local support groups. It's totally okay to ask for help when you need it.

Homesickness

Homesickness is a common part of the college or university experience. While you can't always get rid of it, here are some tips to help manage those waves of longing:

- **Keep in touch with loved ones**: Regular phone calls, video chats, or even just texting can help you feel connected. Let your friends and family know when you're feeling down—they'll want to support you.
- **Make new friends**: It might be uncomfortable at first, but pushing through that initial awkwardness will be worth it. Join clubs, attend events, and engage in activities that interest you. Many other people are also looking to make friends, and you'll find your circle soon enough.
- **Create a sense of home**: Surround yourself with familiar things from home. Photos, souvenirs, or even a favorite blanket can help make your new space feel more comfortable and cozy.
- **Give yourself time**: Homesickness often comes and goes, but it usually gets easier with time. Allow yourself to feel what you're feeling. Journaling or practicing mindfulness can help you focus on the positives of your new adventure and remind you why you're there.

Moving Forward, Step by Step

Deciding what to do after school is a big decision. Take the time to consider your options, and let your personal values and aspirations guide you. Whether it's further academic study, vocational training, or taking time out, there's no right or wrong answer — only what's best for you.

Key Takeaways

- Many paths can lead to success.
- Consider your goals and values when choosing.
- Research your options thoroughly.
- Remember, you can change direction later.

Moving Forward

Whatever path you choose after school, you'll need career skills to succeed. The next chapter will explore strategies for starting and maintaining a successful career.

LAUNCHING YOUR CAREER: NAVIGATING OPPORTUNITIES AND GROWTH

"Whatever you are, be a good one."
— Abraham Lincoln

Think about your first day at a new school or starting a new hobby. Remember that mix of excitement and nervousness you felt? Starting your career brings similar feelings. Whether you've chosen college, an apprenticeship, or jumping straight into work, you'll need to know how to present yourself professionally and grow in your chosen field.

Before we explore how to launch your career, take a moment to reflect:

- What achievements and experiences could you include in a resume?
- How confident do you feel about job interviews?
- Do you know how to find opportunities in your chosen field?
- What does career growth mean to you?

Crafting Your Story: Building a Powerful Resume and Landing Interviews

Have you ever wondered why some people seem to land interviews easily, while others struggle? Often, it comes down to how they present themselves on paper. Your resume (or CV) is like a personal advertisement — it needs to make employers want to know more about you.

BUILDING A STRONG RESUME

Employers often spend less than a minute reviewing each resume, so yours needs to stand out. That means tailoring your resume for each position, highlighting relevant skills and experience.

Your resume needs:
- Clear contact details
- A brief personal statement
- Education history
- Work and volunteer experience
- Key skills
- References

Keep it clean, simple, and error-free. One page is ideal — two pages maximum.

Resume Checklist

- Clear contact information at the top
- Professional email address
- No spelling/grammar errors
- Specific achievements (not just duties)
- Keywords from job descriptions
- Consistent formatting
- Appropriate length (one to two pages)
- Relevant experience highlighted

Need improvements? Focus on areas where you didn't check the box.

MICHAEL SMITH

A motivated and enthusiastic individual with a strong work ethic and a passion for learning.

CONTACT

- ☏ (555) 123-4567
- ✉ msmith@gmail.com
- ⚲ 123 Maple Street | Springfield, IL 62704

KEY SKILLS

- Communication
- Teamwork
- Technical Skills
- Time Management
- Adaptability

REFERENCES

Mr. John Albert Stuart
Manager, SuperMart
(555) 987-6543
JAStuart@supermart.com

Ms. Jane Smith
Volunteer Coordinator,
Springfield Public Library
(555) 765-4321
JSmith@SFlibrary.org

EDUCATION

Springfield High School
High School Diploma | May 2024
- GPA: 3.8/4.0
- Relevant Coursework: Computer Science, Business Studies, Art

WORK EXPERIENCE

Retail Assistant
SuperMart, Springfield, IL
June 2023 – Present
- Increased sales by 10% through upselling and personalized product recommendations.
- Enhanced communication skills by interacting with diverse customers and team members.

Library Volunteer
Springfield Public Library, Springfield, IL
January 2022 – May 2023
- Organized books and assisted patrons with finding resources efficiently.
- Improved time management and problem-solving abilities through multitasking responsibilities.

Tailoring Your Resume

Think of your resume like your outfit — you adjust it depending on where you're going. When applying for jobs:

- Match your skills to what they're asking for.
- Use keywords from the job description.
- Highlight relevant experience.
- Remove irrelevant information and proofread your resume before submission.

WRITING THE PERFECT COVER LETTER

Your cover letter is your first chance to wow a potential employer. In it, you'll introduce yourself and briefly explain why you're a perfect fit for the role.

- Do your research about the company.
- Introduce yourself clearly.
- Share specific examples of your skills.
- Finish strong with enthusiasm for the role.
- Keep it to one page.
- Proofread carefully.

January 26, 2025

Ms. Samantha Alberts
Innovate Solutions
456 Elm Street
Springfield, IL 62705

Dear Ms. Alberts,

I am excited to apply for the Customer Service Associate role at Innovate Solutions. As a recent high school graduate with strong communication, teamwork, and adaptability skills, I bring a proven track record of delivering results.

At SuperMart, I increased sales by 10% through personalized recommendations. Additionally, my volunteer work at Springfield Public Library improved my organizational abilities by streamlining their cataloging system, boosting efficiency by 15%.

I admire Innovate Solutions' dedication to cutting-edge technology and improving customer experiences, and I am confident my skills align with your goals. I look forward to discussing how I can support your success.

Thank you for considering my application.

Sincerely,

Michael Smith
msmith@gmail.com | (555) 123-4567

Getting Noticed: How to Stand Out in a Competitive Job Market

The job market is extremely competitive, so it's crucial to ensure your applications stand out. Beyond having the right skills, you also need to:

- **Follow application instructions precisely**: If they ask for specific details or submission methods, follow them exactly. Missing these details can lead to immediate rejection.
- **Apply early in the application period**: Submitting your application when positions first open shows initiative and ensures you're considered before the employer gets overwhelmed with applications.
- **Use keywords from the job description**: Many companies use software to scan applications. Including relevant terms from the job posting helps your application make it through this first screening.
- **Perfect your online presence**: Ensure your LinkedIn profile or online portfolio is up to date and professional. Many employers will check these.
- **Network and build contacts**: Jobs are often filled through connections before they're even advertised. Attend industry events, join professional groups, and don't be shy about talking to people in your field.
- **Follow up professionally**: A brief, polite follow-up email a week after applying shows initiative and interest without being pushy.

Navigating the Job Search: Applications, Interviews, and Negotiations

"Start where you are. Use what you have. Do what you can."
—**Arthur Ashe**

Finding a job can be both exciting and challenging. Whether you're looking for your first part-time role or starting your career, knowing where and how to look makes a big difference.

WHERE TO FIND OPPORTUNITIES

Though competition can be tough, there are more ways than ever to find jobs:

Online Platforms:

- Set up profiles on key sites like LinkedIn and Indeed.
- Create job alerts for positions that interest you.
- Follow companies you'd like to work for.

Direct Applications:

- Check company websites regularly.
- Sign up for their talent networks.
- Follow their social media for announcements.

Networking:

- Share your career interests with family and friends.
- Attend industry events and job fairs.
- Join professional groups in your field.

How to Shine in Interviews

Do interviews make you feel a little anxious? That's totally normal! But just like preparing for a test or performance, the right preparation will help you feel confident and do your best.

Before the Interview:

- Research the company — know what they do and why you want to work there.
- Practice answering common questions with a friend or family member.
- Plan what to wear and how to get there.
- Get a good night's sleep.

During the Interview:

- Listen carefully to questions.
- It's okay to take a moment to think before answering.
- Share examples of things you've achieved.
- Ask questions about the role and company.

After the Interview:

- Send a thank you email within 24 hours.
- Follow up if you haven't heard back within a week.
- Don't stop your job search — keep looking until you have a firm offer.
- Learn from each interview experience.

Are You Interview Ready?

Think about your best achievement.

- What was the challenge?
- What exactly did you do?
- What was the result?

Practice telling this story in under a minute.

Use the STAR Method

The STAR method helps you organize answers to questions about how you've handled situations, or about personal experiences.

S - SITUATION
Start by describing the context or challenge

"In a group project at school, we struggled to meet a deadline because the team wasn't working well."

T - TASK
Explain your specific role or responsibility

"As the group leader, I was responsible for ensuring we completed the project on time."

A - ACTION
Describe what you did to address the problem

"I created a shared schedule, assigned tasks, and organized meetings to track progress."

R - RESULT
Share the outcome of your actions

"We finished the project on time, and we earned an A Grade."

Negotiating Your Worth

Negotiating a salary is a normal part of working life. As the saying goes, "If you don't ask, you don't get." Being prepared for salary negotiations, starting from the interview stage, is crucial.

- **Research market rates:** Use sites like Glassdoor or Payscale to find out typical salaries for similar roles in your area.
- **Know your value:** Be ready to explain your skills and experience. Don't undersell yourself.
- **Consider the whole package:** Consider benefits like training opportunities, flexible hours, health care, bonuses, and other perks.

- **Stay professional:** Show appreciation while being clear about what you want.
- **Get it in writing:** Make sure any agreements are documented.

Earning Promotions

Promotions and raises are an exciting part of working life. While they sometimes happen without you asking, you'll usually need to take the initiative.

- **Excel in your current role:** Do your current job really well.
- **Go the extra mile:** Look for ways to exceed expectations and add value.
- **Make your achievements known:** Keep track of your successes.
- **Ask when the time is right:** Choose a good moment to discuss your advancement.

Managing Workplace Dynamics: Navigating Challenges and Building Success

The workplace is like a small community filled with different personalities and ways of working. Learning to navigate these relationships professionally is key to your success.

Communication Across Cultures

Workplaces today often bring together people from many backgrounds. Show respect for differences and be open to learning from others. Sometimes this means:

- Being aware of different communication styles
- Avoiding slang or complex expressions
- Showing respect for different perspectives
- Asking questions when you're unsure

Setting Professional Boundaries

It's important to be helpful and flexible at work, but also to maintain healthy boundaries:

- Be clear about your working hours.
- Learn to say no professionally.
- Take your breaks.
- Keep work relationships professional.

Maintaining a Professional Image

Your professional image isn't just about how you dress — it's about how you present yourself overall:

- Be reliable — do what you say you'll do.
- Be on time.
- Keep your commitments.
- Stay positive and constructive.

- Think before you post on social media.
- Communicate professionally in emails and messages.

Handling Conflict

Unfortunately, not every work situation will be positive. Knowing how to handle difficult situations professionally is an important skill.

When conflicts arise:

- Stay calm and professional.
- Focus on finding solutions.
- Listen to other viewpoints.
- Ask for help from your colleagues, manager, or HR team (if needed).
- Document serious issues.

Bullying

Sometimes, workplace issues can be more serious and go beyond normal conflicts. Bullying can take many forms — from constant criticism to exclusion or intimidation. If you experience or witness bullying, know that it's not okay and you don't have to handle it alone. Keep a record of what's happening and don't be afraid to talk to your manager, HR, or someone you trust about the situation.

Key points to remember:

- Address issues professionally and directly, when possible.
- Document serious problems.
- Know your rights.
- Seek help, when needed.

EMBRACING CHANGE

Change is constant in today's workplace. Being adaptable helps you grow and thrive. Think of change as an opportunity to learn new skills and try new approaches. Stay positive and open-minded, but don't be afraid to ask questions when you need clarity. Supporting others through changes while managing your own adjustment shows real professional maturity.

Key points for handling change:

- Stay positive but realistic.
- Be ready to learn new things.
- Ask questions when needed.
- Support others through transitions.
- See challenges as opportunities for growth.

Your Career, Your Future

Starting your career is an exciting journey. Whether you're pursuing further education, beginning an apprenticeship, or heading straight into work, the professional skills in this chapter will help you make a strong start and build positive workplace relationships.

KEY TAKEAWAYS

- Present yourself professionally from day one.
- Prepare thoroughly for opportunities.
- Build positive workplace relationships.
- Manage conflicts professionally.
- Keep learning and growing.
- Remember that change brings opportunity.

MOVING FORWARD

You now have the tools to start building your professional reputation and navigate workplace dynamics. But a successful career needs a stable foundation in your personal life, too. The next chapter explores creating your own space, from finding housing to managing transportation.

BUILDING YOUR OWN SPACE: NAVIGATING HOUSING, ROOMMATES, AND TRANSPORTATION

"Take the first step in faith. You don't have to see the whole staircase, just take the first step."
— **Martin Luther King Jr.**

The thought of having your own space — whether it's a dorm room, shared house, or apartment — is exciting. It's a big step toward independence, but it also comes with new responsibilities. From finding the right place to live to figuring out how to get around, there's a lot to think about.

Before we begin, take a moment to reflect:

- What kind of living space would suit you best?
- How do you feel about sharing your space with others?
- What transportation options are available in your area?
- What new responsibilities are you ready to take on?

From Apartment Hunting to Renting Smart: Finding Your Rental Home

Renting is often your first step into independent living. When you rent, you pay a monthly amount to use someone else's property as your home. Like any big decision, it helps to understand the basics before you start looking.

What to Know About Renting

When you rent a place, you'll pay monthly to a landlord (the owner) or their agent. Let's look at the benefits and challenges of renting:

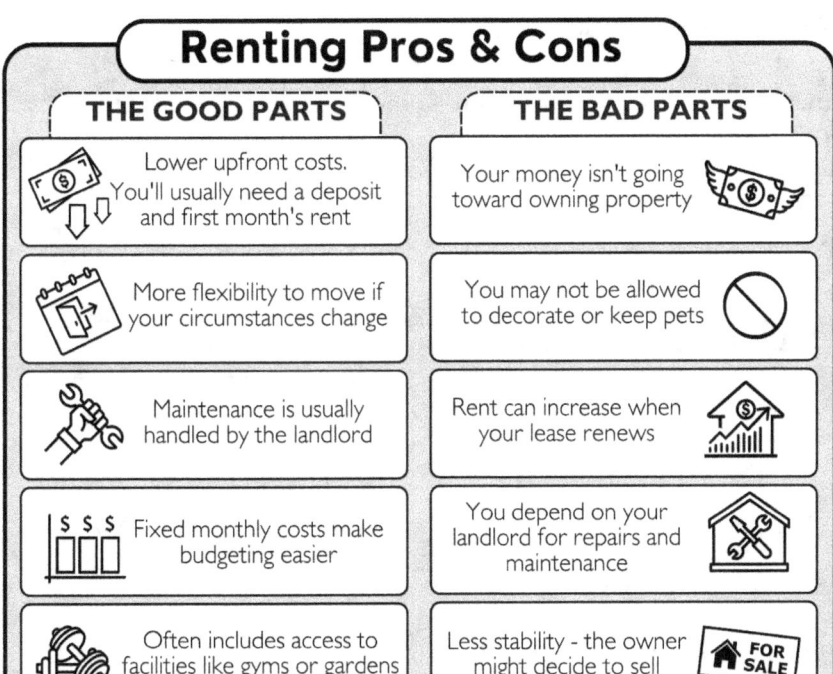

Types of Rental Options

Your first rental might be:

- A room in a shared house
- A studio apartment
- A small apartment or flat
- Student housing

Renting Solo vs Sharing

Living alone gives you complete control over your space, but it costs more. Sharing with others can save money and be more social, but requires good communication and compromise.

Finding Your First Rental

Looking for your first place can feel overwhelming, but breaking it down into steps makes it easier.

Start Your Search:

- Use rental websites and apps.
- Check local real estate agents.
- Look at university housing boards.
- Ask friends and family for recommendations.
- Search local community groups.

What to Consider:

- Location: Think about distance to work/study.
- Budget: Remember that rent isn't your only cost.
- Safety: Research the neighborhood.
- Transportation: Check available options.
- Condition: Look for signs of any obvious problems.

When Viewing Properties:

- Take photos (ask permission first).
- Check water pressure and heating.
- Look for signs of dampness or mold.
- Test light switches and power outlets.
- Check phone signal and Internet options.
- Open windows and cupboards.
- Look carefully at shared areas.

Red Flags to Watch For:

- Landlord pressuring you to decide quickly
- Property in poor condition
- Unclear terms about deposits or fees
- Unwillingness to make repairs
- Bad reviews from previous tenants

Navigating the Rental Application Process

After you find a rental property you like, before you can move in, you'll usually need to provide:

- Proof of ID
- Proof of income or support
- References
- Credit report
- Security deposit
- First month's rent

Your Rental Agreement

Once you've provided all the necessary paperwork and been accepted, it's time to check and sign the rental agreement. This rental agreement, or lease, outlines the terms between you and your landlord. Make sure you understand:

- How much rent you'll pay
- When rent is due
- Length of the lease
- Deposit details
- Maintenance responsibilities
- Rules about guests and noise
- How to end the lease

Building a Positive Relationship with Your Landlord

Having a good relationship with your landlord makes renting smoother and much easier. It's like any relationship — mutual respect, communication, and cooperation are the secrets to success.

- Pay rent on time.
- Report issues promptly.
- Follow the property rules.
- Keep the place clean and tidy.
- Get permission before making changes.

Sharing Space: Maintaining Good Roommate Dynamics and Communication

Living with others can be fun and help cut costs, but it takes good communication and respect to make it work. Whether you're sharing with friends or new people, there are a few ways to make it successful.

FINDING COMPATIBLE ROOMMATES

Think carefully about who you live with:

- Be clear about your living style.
- Discuss expectations about cleaning and guests.
- Talk about schedules and noise.
- Agree on sharing bills and groceries.
- Make sure everyone can afford their share.

Checking Compatibility

Before committing to live with someone, have an honest conversation about your living needs and expectations. Discuss cleaning standards and chore division, quiet hours and sleep schedules, policies around guests and overnight visitors, how you'll share bills and household supplies, and any rules about pets. Aligning on these crucial factors before moving in helps prevent future conflicts.

Quick Roommate Compatibility

Before agreeing to live with someone, ask yourself these questions:

- **What's your ideal living space like?**
    A. Always neat and organized
    B. Generally tidy, with some clutter
    C. Relaxed about mess
- **How do you feel about noise?**
    A. Need quiet most of the time
    B. Okay with regular conversation/music
    C. Love a lively atmosphere
- **What about guests?**
    A. Prefer few visitors
    B. Fine with occasional guests
    C. Love having people over
- **How do you handle shared costs?**
    A. Track everything exactly
    B. Split things roughly equally
    C. Relaxed about sharing

What Your Answers Mean:

Mostly A's: You prefer structure and might be happiest with similarly organized roommates.

Mostly B's: You're flexible and could adapt to different living styles.

Mostly C's: You're laid back and might suit a more social living situation.

Effective Communication and Conflict Resolution

Living with others requires open, honest communication. Think of it like being part of a small team — everyone needs to work together to create a comfortable home. When issues come up, address them early and calmly. A small problem discussed right away is better than letting frustrations build up.

Thinking Beyond Rent: Exploring Home Ownership

While renting is often the first step toward independent living, understanding home ownership helps you plan for the future. Let's explore what this means.

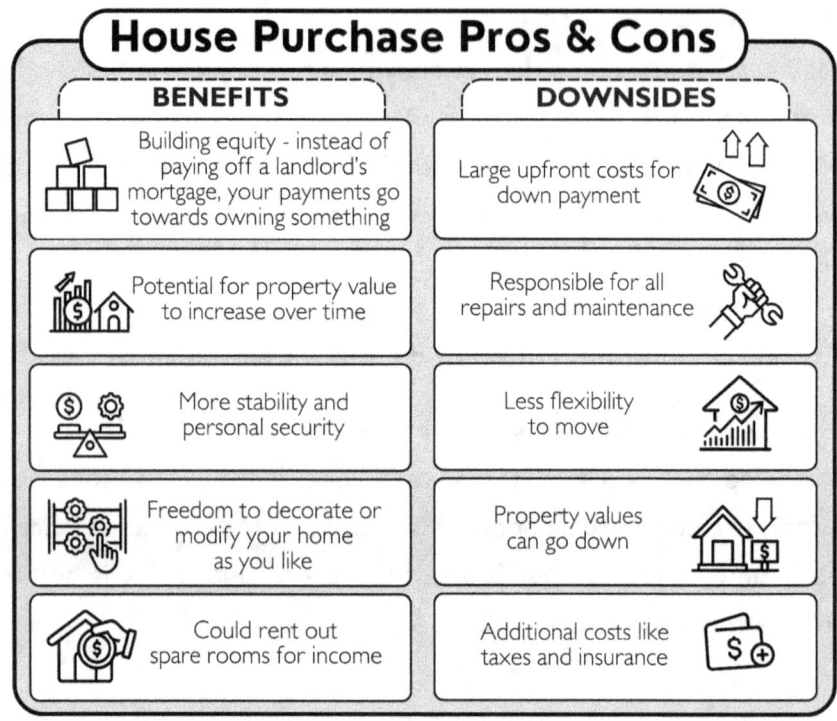

Understanding Mortgages

A mortgage is a loan designed specifically for buying property. When you take out a mortgage, you agree to make regular monthly payments to the lender until the loan is fully repaid. Mortgages typically fall into two categories.

Fixed-Rate Mortgages

- The interest rate stays the same throughout the loan term.
- Factors such as market conditions, the loan term, and your credit score determine the interest rate.
- Payments remain predictable over time.
- Usually run for 15-30 years.
- A good option when interest rates are low, providing long-term stability.

Adjustable-Rate Mortgages (ARM)

- The interest rate is fixed for an initial period, after which it can go up or down.
- After the fixed period, the interest rate adjusts based on external market factors.
- Monthly payments may vary.
- Often starts with lower initial payments, making it more affordable.
- Can be more cost-effective initially, but riskier in the long term due to potential increases.

Down Payments

Unless you're lucky enough to afford to purchase a property outright, you'll likely need to make a down payment or deposit to secure your mortgage. Lenders often require a minimum down payment (typically around 20%, though this can vary). A larger deposit can reduce your monthly mortgage payments and overall loan costs.

Are You Ready to Purchase a Home?

Buying a home is a big financial commitment, so it's essential to prepare carefully. Start by evaluating your finances:
- **Income**: Ensure your earnings can support a mortgage and other associated costs.
- **Savings**: Check if you have enough for a down payment and additional expenses like closing costs or moving fees.
- **Credit Score**: A good credit score can help you secure better mortgage terms.
- **Debts**: Review outstanding debts to understand their impact on your borrowing capacity.

Once you have a clear picture of your financial health, research the housing market and homeownership options.

- **Property Prices**: Explore prices in your preferred location to set realistic expectations.
- **Mortgage Options**: Compare different types of mortgages and interest rates to find the best fit. At this point, you may need to consult a financial advisor.
- **Payment Assistance Programs**: Check for government schemes or grants that might ease your financial burden.

By this stage, you should have a good understanding of what you can afford and the choices available. For additional help, consider consulting a financial advisor to ensure you're making smart and informed decisions.

Dialing in Transportation: Getting Around

Wherever you live, you'll need to figure out how to get around. The best option for you will depend on your lifestyle, budget, and local transportation options.

USING PUBLIC TRANSPORTATION

Public transportation is often cheaper and more eco-friendly than driving. Look into travel passes, which often save money compared to single tickets. Don't forget to check for discounts, like student rates.

WALKING

For short trips, walking is a great option. It's completely free, keeps you active, and helps you explore your neighborhood.

CYCLING

If you're in a city, cycling can be a fast and fun way to get around. It's healthy, and you won't have to worry about parking.

Ride-Sharing and Carpooling

Ride-sharing apps and carpooling with friends or coworkers are good ways to save cash and be kind to the planet. Talk to your classmates or roommates to see if you can share rides regularly.

Owning a Vehicle

If public transport isn't great where you live, owning a car might be your best option. But keep in mind that cars are expensive, and the costs go beyond just buying one.

Obtaining a Driver's License

To drive, you'll need a license. The process depends on where you live, but usually includes lessons, a written test, and a driving exam. Check your local government website to find out what you need to do.

The Cost of Vehicle Ownership

Cars come with ongoing expenses, so make sure you're ready for them. Typical expenses include:

- The price of the car itself
- Fuel
- Insurance (this can be pricey for young drivers!)

- Taxes and registration
- Maintenance and repairs
- Parking fees

Do some research to figure out what these costs will be in your area, and build a buffer into your budget for those unpleasant surprises, like repairs.

Where to Buy a Car

There are several options for buying a vehicle, each with its pros and cons.

Car Purchase Pros & Cons

OPTIONS	PROS	CONS
BUYING NEW	Brand-new car, warranty, no concerns about past issues.	Expensive, and it loses value quickly.
BUYING USED	Cheaper upfront, less depreciation, and often lower insurance costs.	You might run into hidden problems, and repairs could be more frequent.
LEASING	Lower monthly payments and access to a new car.	You don't own the car, and there are limits on how much you can drive.

Time to Get Moving!

Stepping into independence is an exciting milestone, and managing your housing, roommates, and transportation are important pieces of the life puzzle. By making informed decisions, you'll set yourself up for a smoother transition to adulthood.

KEY TAKEAWAYS

- Renting offers flexibility, but comes with responsibilities.
- Sharing a living space requires clear communication and compromise.
- Transportation options depend on your lifestyle, budget, and location.
- Owning a car involves significant ongoing costs, so plan carefully.

MOVING FORWARD

Now that you understand how to create your own space, it's time to focus on managing your money. The next chapter covers everything from budgeting to credit, loans, and saving for the future. Get ready to take control of your finances and build a solid foundation!

BUILDING FINANCIAL STRENGTH: MANAGING MONEY FOR YOUR FUTURE

"I hope the way you spend your money is in line with the truth of who you are and what you care about."
— **Oprah Winfrey**

How do you handle money? Are you a saver, a spender, or someone who avoids thinking about it altogether? No matter your approach, learning to manage your finances is a vital life skill that can set you on the path to achieving your goals and living the life you want.

Before we begin, take a moment and ask yourself:

- How confident do you feel about managing money?
- What are your biggest money questions or concerns?
- What financial goals would you like to achieve?
- How do you want your relationship with money to look?

Budgeting Basics: Controlling Expenses and Saving Wisely

Budgeting is the foundation of smart money management. **The concept is simple: Track what comes in, control what goes out, and save for the future.** A good budget not only prevents you from overspending, but also helps you plan for both immediate needs and long-term goals.

Key Steps to Effective Budgeting:

- **Track your income and expenses**: Write down every expense, no matter how small. Use tools like notebooks, spreadsheets, or budgeting apps such as YNAB, Goodbudget, or GNUCash to stay organized.
- **Allocate funds for priorities**: Focus on essentials like rent, utilities, and groceries first.
- **Avoid overspending**: Make sure your total expenses stay below your income.

Choosing a Budgeting Method

There isn't a one-size-fits-all budget. Find a system that works for your personality, priorities, and financial situation — or combine strategies to create your own.

- **50/30/20 Rule:** Divide your income into three categories:
    - **50% needs**: Housing, bills, groceries
    - **30% wants**: Entertainment, dining out, etc.
    - **20% savings**: Emergency fund, future goals
      This method balances essential expenses with enjoying life and planning for the future.
- **Pay Yourself First:** Prioritize savings by automatically transferring a set amount from your income (eg. 10–20%) into savings before spending on anything else.
- **Envelope System:** Put cash in labeled envelopes for things like food or going out. Spend only what's in each envelope — once your 'eating out' envelope is empty, it's time for instant noodles at home!

Money Mindset Moment

Managing money and sticking to a budget starts with awareness — knowing exactly what's coming in and what's going out. Take this quick exercise:

1. Write down your last three purchases.

2. Label each as either a **need** or a **want**.

3. Look at the list: Is there one purchase you could have skipped?

This simple reflection helps you understand your spending habits and shows where you might find opportunities to save. Small changes can lead to big financial wins!

ESSENTIAL EXPENSES AND OTHER PRIORITIES

Managing your finances starts with focusing on the essentials. These are the foundational expenses that keep your life running smoothly, including:

- **Housing Costs**: Rent or mortgage payments
- **Utilities**: Water, electricity, gas, and Internet
- **Groceries**: Food and necessary household items

- **Health Care**: Prescriptions, medical appointments, and insurance
- **Insurance**: Car, home, health, or other coverage
- **Essential Travel**: Public transportation, car payments, fuel, or bike maintenance
- **Debt Repayments**: Loans, credit card payments, or other debts

Once your essential needs are met, prioritize saving before spending on non-essential "wants." Remember: **Save first, spend later**.

Paying Your Bills

Bills are unavoidable, but managing them effectively makes life easier. Here are some tips to stay on top of payments.

- **Automate payments:** Set up auto-pay for recurring bills to avoid late fees.
- **Set reminders:** Use apps or your calendar to alert you to upcoming due dates.
- **Audit regularly:** Review your subscriptions and recurring services to cut unnecessary costs. These small regular payments are often opportunities to save. Ask yourself tough questions:
  - "Do I really use that gym membership, or could I workout at home?"
  - "Is my streaming subscription worth it, or am I paying for shows I never watch?"

Finding Affordable Options

Getting the most value for your money is an essential skill that can make budgeting both easier and more rewarding. Here are some strategies to help you save without sacrificing quality:

- **Do your research.**
  Before making a purchase, compare options. Look at different brands, prices, and reviews to ensure you're getting the best value.

- Don't just go for the cheapest option. Instead, consider durability, repairability, and resale value.
- Compare prices online and in store — sometimes, local stores have unexpected deals.

- **Look for sales and discounts.**
Plan big purchases around sales like Black Friday or Boxing Day. End-of-season sales are ideal for items like clothing or accessories.

- **Use price comparison sites.**
Websites like **Google Shopping** and **PriceGrabber** can help you compare prices across multiple retailers. Regularly updated, these tools make finding the best price easier.

- **Buy second-hand or refurbished.**
Thrift stores, online marketplaces, and garage sales are treasure troves for second-hand finds. For electronics, consider refurbished options from trusted dealers — they often come with warranties and cost much less than new items.

- **Buy in bulk.**
Non-perishable items and household essentials are often cheaper in bulk.
  - Share memberships to bulk retailers like Costco with friends or family for additional savings.
  - Make sure you have enough storage space to accommodate bulk buys.

> **Reflection Questions:**
> - What steps could you take today to save money or cut out unnecessary spending?
> - Is there anything you could buy second-hand instead of new?
> - What items do you regularly use that you could buy in bulk to save money?

Savings Made Simple

"Any fool can spend money. But to earn it and save it and defer gratification — then you learn to value it differently."
— **Malcolm Gladwell**

Saving is a crucial part of a healthy financial life. Once you've covered your essential expenses, saving should be your next focus. The key is **consistency**: Even small, regular contributions add up over time.

TYPES OF SAVINGS

Think of your savings as separate "money pots" — each serving a different purpose. This helps you track and meet specific goals.

There are four basic pots: emergency fund, short-term goals (like a vacation), long-term goals (like a home), and retirement. Don't stress about setting up all four immediately. Start with just one savings goal — like setting aside $500 for emergencies or something you really want. Once you hit that goal, you can build on it or create new ones — what matters most is beginning to save.

1. Emergency Fund: This is your safety net for unexpected genuine emergency expenses, like medical bills or car repairs.

- Start with $500 to cover surprises like a flat tire or a broken phone. Once you hit that, aim for three to six months' worth of expenses.
- Keeping this money in a standard savings account allows you quick access.

2. Short-Term Savings: This is for goals you plan to achieve in the next five years, like a vacation, a new laptop, or a special event.

- Consider fixed-term savings accounts for better interest rates. These accounts often provide better interest rates in exchange for keeping your money locked in for a set period, typically from six months to several years.
- Ensure the money is separate from daily spending.

3. Long-Term Savings: This fund is for bigger goals, like buying a house or starting a business.

- Try to add to this fund steadily over time.
- Look for high-yield, fixed-term savings accounts — they offer better interest rates than standard accounts, but limit access to the money.
- Resist the urge to dip into it for other expenses.

4. Retirement: Retirement might seem a long way off right now, but saving early gives your money more time to grow. The earlier you begin, the more you benefit from compound interest.

Interest and Compounding

What Is Interest?
Interest is the percentage you earn on top of your savings (or that you pay on loans). Think of it as the cost of borrowing money or the reward for saving it.

The Power of Compound Interest
Compound interest is like a snowball rolling down a hill — it grows faster the longer it rolls. Start saving early, and even small amounts will add up over time.

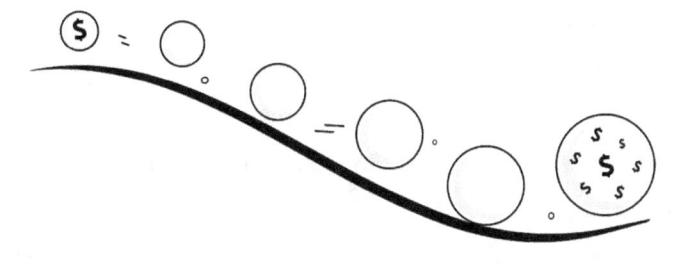

The Compounding Snowball Effect

Here's how it works:
- **Starting Amount:** $1,000
- **Monthly Contribution:** $100
- **Annual Interest Rate:** 5%

Look at how your money grows:
- **After 1 Year:** $2,284. (You've contributed $2,200)
- **After 5 Years:** $8,112. (You've contributed $7,000)
- **After 10 Years:** $17,239. (You've contributed $13,000)
- **After 20 Years:** $43,987. (You've contributed $25,000)

This example illustrates the exponential growth effect of compounding.

The Keys to Successful Saving

- **Start early:** The sooner you start, the more time compounding has to work its magic. Even small amounts can grow significantly over time.
- **Be consistent:** Regular contributions, even if small, are crucial. Skipping deposits can slow your progress. While $20/month may not seem like much, it builds a habit and will grow over time.
- **Don't interrupt the process:** Withdrawing money interrupts the compounding process, so try to leave your savings untouched unless absolutely necessary.
- **Automate your savings:** Set up automatic transfers on payday. Treat savings like any other essential bill.
- **Save windfalls:** When you receive unexpected money (like gifts or bonuses), save at least some of it, rather than spending it all.

Savings and Inflation

Saving is crucial, but inflation can reduce your money's value over time — something no one wants.

What Is Inflation?

Imagine you love pizza. This year, a slice costs $5. Next year, it might cost $5.25 for the same slice. That's inflation — it makes your money buy less pizza over time!

How **inflation** has changed the Price of a Cup of Coffee over time

1970	1980	1990	2000	2010	2024
=$0.40	=$0.90	=$1.50	=$2.00	=$2.50	=$3.50

To protect your savings from inflation:
- Look for savings accounts with interest rates higher than inflation. Example: If your account earns 4.5% while inflation runs at 2.5%, your money's value grows rather than shrinks.
- Consider other ways to grow your money for long-term goals.
- Remember that emergency funds and short-term savings are less affected, as they're not held as long.

Understanding Debt: Loans, Credit Management, and Building Credit History

In an ideal world, you would never need to borrow money. However, as you get older, debt often becomes a necessary part of life — whether for education, purchasing a home, or starting a business.

What Is Debt?

Debt is money that has been borrowed and that must be repaid, usually with interest. Think of it like hiring a car — you need to return it in good condition and on time, and you pay someone for using it. Common types include:

- Student loans for education
- Mortgages for buying property
- Personal loans for larger purchases
- Credit cards for everyday spending
- "Buy now, pay later" services

Debit Cards vs. Credit Cards

While debit and credit cards may look similar, they function very differently:

- **Credit Cards:** Borrowed money from a lender, which you must repay (often with interest if not paid on time).
- **Debit Cards:** Money comes directly from your bank account. You can only spend what you have (unless you have a prearranged overdraft).

Remember that credit is not "free money," but rather borrowed funds that have to be repaid — usually with interest. Failing to repay can seriously impact your future.

Responsible Borrowing

No matter what type of borrowing you do, it's crucial to do it responsibly. Taking on debt is a big commitment. Before borrowing, always:

- **Know why you're borrowing:**
    - Have a clear purpose.
    - Only borrow what you need (and can afford to repay in full every month).
    - Understand how you'll use the money.
    - Create a realistic repayment plan.

- **Understand the terms:**
  - Know exactly what you're agreeing to.
  - Compare interest rates and fees.
  - Check repayment schedules.
  - Understand free interest periods and penalties for missed payments.

Managing Your Debts

If you know what you're getting into and treat debt responsibly, borrowing can open up opportunities that would otherwise be unavailable (e.g., purchasing a house). The crucial thing is to manage your debt properly. The more debts you have, the trickier they become to manage, so never take on debt unless it serves a real purpose.

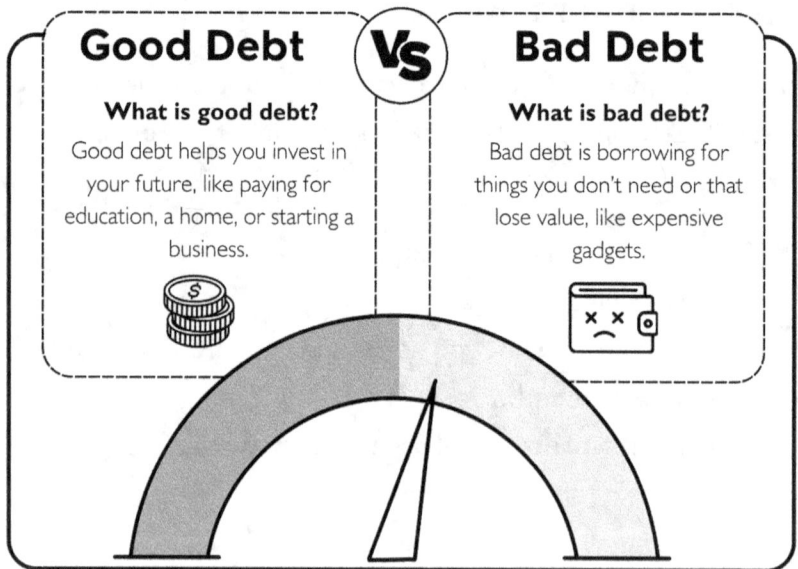

Good Debt vs Bad Debt

What is good debt?
Good debt helps you invest in your future, like paying for education, a home, or starting a business.

What is bad debt?
Bad debt is borrowing for things you don't need or that lose value, like expensive gadgets.

Avoiding High-Interest Debt

If you ever need to borrow money, look for low-interest options, like loans from a bank or credit union. These are much safer than payday loans, which can lead to debt trouble.

STRATEGIES TO STAY DEBT-FREE

- **Avoid unnecessary debt**: Only consider taking on debt for value-adding purposes, such as purchasing a home or investing in your education.
- **Be careful with credit:** Only borrow what you can pay off in full each month. Late payments can lead to mounting fees, especially with credit cards and "buy now, pay later" products like Klarna.
- **Shop around:** Research thoroughly when looking for credit cards, loans, or other financial products. Compare interest rates and terms.
- **Keep your credit score healthy:** Always pay your bills on time to protect and improve your credit score.
- **Stay away from payday lenders:** Short-term payday loans often come with extremely high interest rates and aggressive debt collection practices. They can trap borrowers in a cycle of debt, making them one of the riskiest financial products.
- **Know your limits:** If you find yourself trying to justify a debt to yourself or others, it's a warning sign you might not be able to afford it. Consult a financial advisor if you're uncertain about taking on any debt.

Investing for Your Future: Starting Small and Growing Wealth

Think investing is only for the wealthy? Think again. When done responsibly, investing is a powerful way to grow wealth and protect against inflation. You don't need a lot of money to get started, but you do need to understand what you're doing, as investing recklessly can lead to losses.

The Power of Starting Early

The earlier you start investing, the better. Small amounts can grow significantly over time due to compound interest. However, it's never too late to start.

Basic Investment Types

When starting out, focus on the basics and take time to understand the different investment types:

- **Stocks/Shares:** When you buy a stock, you own a small part of a company. The value goes up and down based on how well the company does. It can be exciting, but also risky, since a company's success isn't guaranteed.
- **Funds:** Funds combine money from many investors to buy lots of different stocks. This spreads the risk around, which

can make it safer than buying individual stocks. Professionals usually manage them.
- **Bonds:** Buying a bond means lending money to a company or government. In return, you get interest. It's a safer bet, but with smaller rewards.

Understanding Your Goals and Risk Tolerance

Investing works best when aligned with your goals. Consider if you're looking for short-term growth or long-term security. Also, understand how much risk you're willing to take. A financial advisor can help create a personalized investment plan based on your situation and goals.

- **Short-Term Goals:** For beginners, short-term investing is risky. Savings accounts with good interest rates are usually a better option.
- **Long-Term Goals:** Investing for the long term can help grow wealth steadily. Diversifying through funds can provide stable returns over time.
- **Risk Tolerance:**
  - Decide how much you're willing to risk for potential gains.
  - Never invest more than you can afford to lose.
  - Consider mixing investments with different risk levels.
  - Remember that higher risk doesn't guarantee higher returns.

Investing and Tax

Remember that investment profits are generally taxable. Examples include:

- **Capital Gains Tax:** Tax on profit from selling an investment.
- **Dividend Tax:** Tax on dividends earned from investments.
- **Interest Income Tax:** Tax on interest earned.

Make sure to understand the tax implications of investing in your country before making any decisions.

Financial Planning for the Long Term

While the present often feels more urgent, financial planning is about preparing for the future. The sooner you start saving and investing, the more secure and comfortable your later years will be. You don't need to be wealthy to start investing — even small, regular contributions can grow significantly over time.

Exploring Retirement Accounts

Retirement accounts, like pensions, are essential for long-term financial security. Options vary by country, but many governments and employers contribute to employee pensions. Common types include:

- 401(k)/403(b) plans (US)
- Individual Retirement Accounts (IRAs)
- NEST Pensions (UK)
- Superannuation (Australia)

Taking Care of Taxes

Taxes fund essential public services and are a key part of living in society. Depending on where you live, taxes may:

- Be deducted automatically from your income
- Be filed by the individual
- Need different handling if you're self-employed

Tax rates often increase with income, so understanding your tax obligations is crucial. If your situation is complex or you're self-employed, consider consulting a tax professional.

INSURING FOR THE FUTURE

Insurance protects you against unexpected events that could lead to financial losses. In return for paying an insurance company a monthly premium, they agree to cover you for specific scenarios. Common types of insurance include:

- **Health Insurance:** Covers medical expenses like hospital stays and prescriptions. It may be mandatory or optional, depending on where you live.
- **Home Insurance:** Protects your home and its contents against disasters, damage, or theft.
- **Vehicle Insurance:** Covers accidents, damage, or theft of your vehicle. Often mandatory.
- **Travel Insurance:** Provides coverage for losses or injuries while traveling.
- **Life Insurance:** Pays a sum to your beneficiaries in the event of your death.

> **Quick Finance Check:**
>
> 1. What's the difference between a debit and credit card?
> 2. How does compound interest work?
> 3. What's an emergency fund?
> 5. What's the purpose of insurance?

Embracing Your Financial Future

A healthy financial situation is a key part of a happy and successful life. Whether you're just starting to save or thinking about investing, the habits you build now will serve you well throughout your life.

Key Takeaways

- Good money management starts with budgeting.
- Save consistently, even if it's small amounts.
- Understand debt before taking it on.
- Start thinking about long-term financial goals.
- Protection through insurance matters.

Moving Forward

Now that you understand how to manage your money, let's look at how to stay safe and smart in the digital world. The next chapter explores managing your online presence, protecting your information, and using digital tools effectively.

MASTERING DIGITAL TOOLS FOR YOUR LIFE: STAYING SAFE AND SMART ONLINE

"The advance of technology is based on making it fit in so that you don't really even notice it, so it's part of everyday life."
— ***Bill Gates***

Think about how much of your life involves technology. From socializing and studying to banking and shopping, the digital world is woven into almost everything we do. While this brings amazing opportunities, it also means we need to be smart about how we use it.

Before we dive in, take a moment to reflect:
- How much of your life happens online?
- Do you know how to protect your digital information?
- What worries you about your online presence?
- How confident are you with digital security?

Protecting Yourself in a Digital World

Not too long ago, the Internet felt like a smaller, safer space. Today, with the explosion of social media, AI, and digital everything, online threats have multiplied. Staying safe means understanding what threats exist and knowing how to protect yourself against them.

Understanding Cyber Threats

Cybercrime covers a wide range of illegal online activities, usually involving theft or deception. Here are some common threats to be aware of:

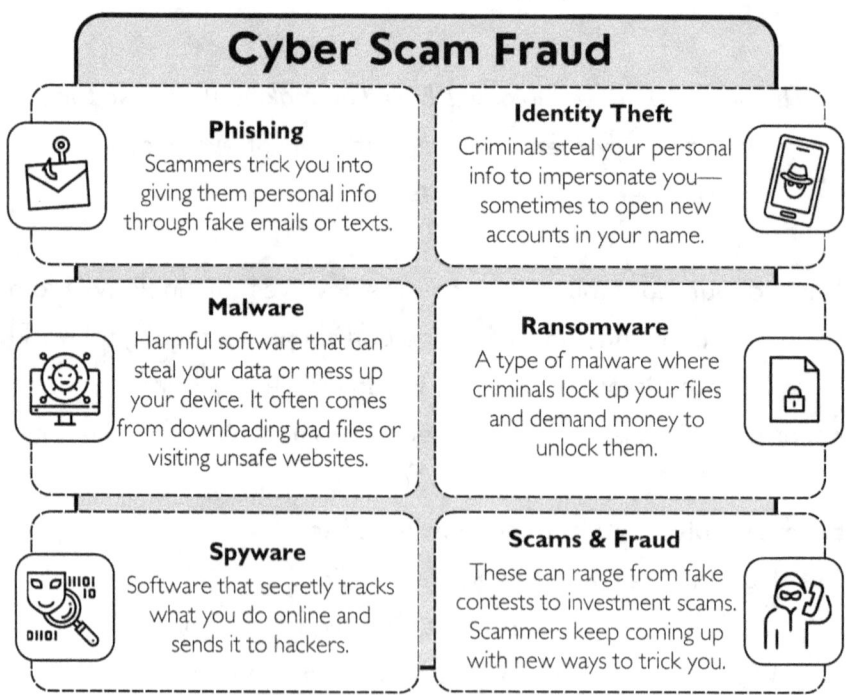

Cyber Scam Fraud

Phishing
Scammers trick you into giving them personal info through fake emails or texts.

Identity Theft
Criminals steal your personal info to impersonate you—sometimes to open new accounts in your name.

Malware
Harmful software that can steal your data or mess up your device. It often comes from downloading bad files or visiting unsafe websites.

Ransomware
A type of malware where criminals lock up your files and demand money to unlock them.

Spyware
Software that secretly tracks what you do online and sends it to hackers.

Scams & Fraud
These can range from fake contests to investment scams. Scammers keep coming up with new ways to trick you.

Protecting Yourself from Cybercrime

Most cybercrime occurs because of simple human errors, like sharing passwords or clicking on suspicious links. Everyone makes mistakes, but you can significantly lower your risk with some simple habits.

Getting Passwords Right

- **Use strong passwords:** Create passwords with a mix of letters, numbers, and symbols. Don't use easy stuff, like your name or birthdate. A password manager can help keep track of them.
- **One password, one account:** Use a different password for each account. That way, if one is stolen, others stay safe.
- **Keep passwords private:** Don't share passwords, even with friends. Don't write them down where others can find them. Consider using a password storage app like LastPass to keep them safe.

Keeping Your Personal Information Safe

You may wonder why privacy matters. The more information you share online, the easier it is for scammers to potentially steal from you.

> ### What Is Personal Information?
>
> Personal information is any data that can identify you, such as your name, phone number, address, login details, and IP address.

Tips for Protecting Your Personal Information:

- **Be cautious about what you share:** Don't give out personal info unless you really need to. Adjust your privacy settings on social media to control who can see what you post.
- **Verify before you share:** Make sure any request for personal info comes from a trusted source. Avoid clicking on links that look suspicious.
- **Use secure websites:** Look for "HTTPS" and a lock symbol before entering personal details. It means the site is secure.

Avoiding Scams

Scams are all over the Internet, but you can spot them with a little awareness:

- **Beware of emails and texts:** Scammers often pretend to be someone you trust to trick you into clicking on links or sharing info. Look for signs like misspellings or strange formatting.

- **If it sounds too good to be true, it probably is:** Be skeptical of offers that seem unreal, like surprise prizes or strange requests from strangers.
- **Don't be rushed:** Scammers often try to make you act quickly by creating a sense of urgency. Slow down and think before you act.

Keeping Your Devices Secure

Keeping your information private is important, but securing your devices is just as vital. Follow these tips to keep your devices safe:

- **Restrict physical access:** Don't let people you don't know use your devices. Even with trusted friends or family, be cautious. Use passwords and make sure to log out when you're not using your devices.
- **Stay up to date:** Install updates as soon as they're available. These updates protect both your software and hardware from known threats.
- **Use a reliable security suite:** Invest in antivirus or security software that does more than just protect against viruses. It should regularly scan your device and alert you to potential threats.
- **Make regular backups:** Back up your system regularly to avoid losing important files. Use both a cloud service and an external hard drive for maximum protection.

Navigating Social Media: Understanding Platforms and Responsible Use

Social media is constantly evolving, offering new ways to connect, share, and express yourself. While social media can be a powerful tool, it's important to use it responsibly.

UNDERSTANDING THE PLATFORMS

Every social media platform has its own strengths. Some focus on visual content (photos and videos), while others focus on text updates or professional networking. Platforms like Facebook, Instagram, TikTok, and YouTube have billions of users, while LinkedIn, Reddit, and Discord cater to specific interests. Keep in mind that social media is constantly changing, so stay informed about new trends and platforms.

SOCIAL MEDIA AND MENTAL HEALTH

Research has linked the use of social media, and particularly its excessive use, with an increase in mental health problems. Try to be aware of the potential negative impacts:

- **Feelings of Inadequacy:** Seeing curated posts can make your life seem dull or make you feel like you're not good enough. **Remember, many people only share their highlights, not the full picture.**

- **Social Withdrawal:** Spending too much time interacting online can make you miss out on real-life connections. It's important to balance online interactions with in-person engagements.
- **Addiction:** Social media platforms are designed to be addictive. Features like autoplay and notifications pull you back into a loop of constant engagement. If you feel anxious without your phone or are constantly checking it, take a break.
- **Harmful Content:** Not all social media content is positive. Harmful, adult, and inappropriate content is widespread. If you come across something that makes you feel uncomfortable, report it to the platform and tell a trusted adult.

Reflect on Your Usage

- How often do you check your social media accounts?
- Have you found yourself comparing your life to what you see online?
- What steps can you take to create a healthier balance?

Showing Respect and Empathy Online

Behind every screen is a real person. Don't let online anonymity lead you to act differently than you would in person. **Treat others with respect and kindness**, even when you disagree. Strive to understand different perspectives and engage thoughtfully.

Dealing with Online Harassment and Cyberbullying

Online harassment and bullying are not behavior you should tolerate. It's crucial to recognize, confront, and call out bullying whenever it occurs — whether online or offline.

Signs of Online Harassment and Cyberbullying

Harassment and cyberbullying involve using online methods to attack or abuse someone. This can happen between peers, coworkers, or strangers. Common signs include:

- Threatening or abusive messages or posts
- Negative or nasty comments
- Spreading lies or rumors
- Sharing someone's private details without permission
- Posting private or altered images or videos
- Excluding someone from a group or conversation

Cyberbullying can have a serious impact on a person's well-being. If you notice it happening, always support the victim and never participate, even if it feels like harmless teasing.

Reporting Harassment and Finding Support

If you're being bullied online, talk to someone you trust — whether that's a friend, family member, or teacher. Next, report the harassment to the platform where it occurred. Most social media sites have tools to report abuse. If threats or safety concerns are involved, contact local authorities for further support.

Responsible Digital Citizenship: Understanding Rights and Responsibilities

Just as living offline comes with rules, rights, and responsibilities, so does being online. Understanding your rights and what is expected of you will help you navigate the digital world safely.

ONLINE DATA AND PRIVACY

The Internet runs on data. Every day, companies gather billions of pieces of data about your online activity — from videos and photos to shopping habits and location. This data can be valuable, which is why many online services are "free."

Companies use this data to create a profile of you and predict your behavior, which helps them target you with ads and offers. It's important to be aware of how your data is being used and shared.

Controlling and Sharing Your Data

You have the right to know who collects your data and how it's used. Before using an app or website, read their privacy policy to understand how your data is handled. Many services allow you to customize what information you share, like turning off location tracking or opting out of targeted ads. Remember, you should always have the option to accept, decline, or withdraw consent.

Cookie Management

Cookies are small files that websites store on your device to track activity. They can help enhance your experience, but they also collect data on your preferences, location, and browsing habits. Websites should notify you about cookie usage and let you choose whether or not to accept certain types.

Cookies are stored fragments of user date used to improve the browsing experience

COOKIE SETTINGS

Pls select which cookies you want to accept.

○ Allow all cookies

○ Only allow first-party cookies

○ Do not allow any cookies

Select an option to continue

App Permissions

When installing an app, remember to review what data it can access — contacts, camera, location, etc. Only grant permissions that are necessary for the app to work. For example, a camera app should be able to access your camera and storage, but doesn't need access to your contacts.

COMBATING FAKE NEWS AND ONLINE MISINFORMATION

Misinformation — often called "fake news" — is widespread online. It's intentionally false content created to mislead people, often for political, social, or financial gain. Here are some ways to protect yourself from misinformation:

- **Practice critical thinking:** Always approach information with skepticism. Don't take things at face value. Look for context and consider the full story. Prioritize reliable sources like government or university websites for accurate information.
- **Check the facts:** Verify information by looking for credible sources or references that confirm or debunk the content. Use trusted fact-checking sites like Snopes, FullFact.org, or FactCheck.org. Be cautious if you can't find supporting evidence from reliable outlets.
- **Think before sharing:** Even if something seems true, double-check before sharing it. Misinformation can be tricky to spot, and everyone is susceptible. Always pause to verify the content before passing it along.

- **Report misinformation:** Most platforms allow users to report false or misleading content. Use these tools to help reduce the spread of misinformation.

Healthy Online Identities: Managing Privacy and Wellness

Just like in other areas of life, it's important to take care of yourself online. This includes your mental well-being, physical health, and reputation.

MANAGING YOUR ONLINE REPUTATION

Everything you post online can impact your reputation and future, so it's important to be proactive. It's easier to manage your reputation now than to try to fix it later when something goes wrong. Keep in mind that what you share today could resurface down the line!

- **Be selective when sharing:** Think about who will see your posts and how they reflect on you. If a post doesn't reflect well on you, don't share it. Also, avoid sharing too much personal information — this can make you vulnerable to identity theft.
- **Compartmentalize:** Separate your personal and professional online spaces. For example, LinkedIn is for professional updates, while Instagram is better for personal photos. Use privacy settings to control who can see your content.

- **Engage wisely and authentically:** Contribute positively online. Think before you post. Consider whether you'd be comfortable with your content being associated with you forever, or seen by your friends and family. Avoid engaging in unnecessary arguments or sharing private matters publicly.
- **Keep information up to date:** Review your online content regularly and remove anything that is outdated or no longer helpful. You can also go back and clean up your old posts.

Maintaining Healthy Digital Boundaries and Habits

Creating a balanced and healthy relationship with the Internet involves setting boundaries that work for you. Here are some tips for staying in control:

- **Manage your screen time:** Social media can suck up a lot of time. Set limits to ensure you prioritize other activities, like eating, sleeping, and exercising. Limiting screen time before bed can also improve your sleep quality.
- **Avoid oversharing:** Be mindful of what you post, as it stays online forever. Avoid posting in the heat of the moment or sharing controversial opinions publicly. Always consider who might see your content and how they could use it.
- **Get the balance right:** Maintain a healthy separation between work or school and personal time. When you're off the clock, don't check emails or work-related messages. Make sure your boundaries are clear and respected.

- **Take regular breaks:** After long periods of device use, take breaks to rest your mind. Stand up, stretch, and move around to refresh both your body and brain.
- **Watch for signs of addiction:** If you're spending endless hours scrolling or feel anxious without your phone, it may be time to take a step back. If it's starting to impact your life, seek help from a trusted adult or health professional.
- **Try a digital detox:** Consider taking breaks from digital technology. A "digital detox" can help you reconnect with the offline world, clear your mind, and find a healthier balance.

Living Well, Both Online and Off

The digital world offers amazing opportunities for connection, learning, and growth, but like any powerful tool, it needs to be used wisely. By understanding both the benefits and risks of technology, you can make the most of digital opportunities while staying safe and healthy.

Key Takeaways

- Protect your digital life with strong passwords and security habits.
- Think before you share — anything posted online can last forever.
- Keep a healthy balance between online and offline activities.
- Stay alert for scams and protect your personal information.
- Remember that your digital reputation matters for your future.

Moving Forward

Now that you know how to navigate the digital world safely, let's focus on taking care of your physical well-being. The next chapter explores how to build and maintain a healthy lifestyle that will serve you well into the future.

PRIORITIZING YOUR HEALTH: BUILDING A STRONG FOUNDATION

"The greatest wealth is health."
— Virgil

When was the last time you truly thought about your health? For many of us, it's easy to ignore until something goes wrong. We tend to forget that our bodies are like any valuable asset — if you don't invest in them, they won't hold up over time. Taking care of your health is far easier than fixing it after it's broken.

Before we begin, take a moment to reflect:

- How do you feel about your current health?
- What healthy habits do you already have?
- What simple steps could you take to improve your health?
- What stops you from making healthier choices?

Preventive Care: Building a Healthy Future

Taking a proactive approach to your health means combining a healthy lifestyle with regular checkups, screenings, and vaccinations.

WHAT IS A HEALTHY LIFESTYLE?

People often talk about living a "healthy lifestyle," but what does that really mean? It's simpler than it sounds, and can be broken down into four key areas:

- **Nutrition**: Food is the foundation of good health. A balanced diet provides essential nutrients for growth and repair, boosts the immune system, and helps prevent illness.
- **Sleep**: Quality sleep supports brain function, emotional regulation, and overall health.
- **Physical Activity**: Humans are built to move. Regular exercise strengthens the muscles, heart, and brain, while also improving mood and energy.

- **Mental Health**: Often overlooked, mental health is just as crucial as physical health. It helps with managing emotions, coping with stress, and overall well-being.

Strategies for Staying Healthy

While Chapter 9 covers nutrition and eating well in detail, this chapter focuses on how to get quality sleep, stay active, and take care of your mental health.

Sleep

Good sleep is a superpower, playing a crucial role in how you feel and function. While everyone's needs are different, most people your age need around eight hours per night. Getting enough restful sleep helps you wake up refreshed, stay focused throughout the day, and make better choices about food and exercise.

Try these tips for better sleep:

- Get morning sunlight to help set your body's internal clock.
- Create a relaxing bedtime routine.
- Keep your bedroom dark and cool.
- Avoid screens in the hour before bed.

> **Sleep Quality Quiz**
>
> Your Sleep Habits:
> - I go to bed at the same time each day.
> - My bedroom is dark and quiet.
> - I avoid screens in the hour before bed.
> - I wake without an alarm.
> - I feel rested in the morning.
>
> Score: ___/5
> 3 or below? Time to improve your sleep hygiene.

Physical Exercise

The human body thrives on movement. Regular physical activity strengthens your muscles, bones, and brain, contributing to overall health. You don't need a gym membership or fancy equipment—just a commitment to move more.

Walking is one of the easiest ways to stay active. Fit it into your routine by taking stairs instead of elevators or getting off the bus one stop early. Find activities you enjoy, whether those include team sports, dancing, or cycling. The best exercise is the one you'll actually do.

Mental Health

Until recently, mental health was often overlooked or misunderstood. Now, we recognize that mental health deserves just as much attention as physical health. Taking care of your mental health doesn't guarantee you won't face challenges — most people experience difficult periods — but it makes you more resilient.

Alongside eating well, sleeping enough, and regular exercise, try these strategies:

- **Practice self-care:** Self-care isn't just about treats or expensive routines. It's about daily activities that make you feel good and healthy — like quiet time alone, reading, walking in nature, or doing things you enjoy.
- **Stay connected:** Humans need social connections to thrive. You don't need a huge circle of friends — just a few people you can rely on during good and bad times. Make sure the people around you are positive influences rather than causing you stress.
- **Develop coping skills:** Building resilience and managing stress are vital skills. Techniques like mindfulness, keeping a regular routine, and recognizing what triggers stress can help you cope with difficult moments. Remember, it's okay to feel your emotions — acknowledge them, then let them pass.

Managing Your Personal Health Needs

Regular check-ups help catch potential issues early. Your primary care doctor or local health care center is usually your first point of contact for general medical care like routine check-ups. For more specialized care, you might visit dentists, opticians, or dermatologists.

Finding Health Care Providers

Health care systems vary by country. For example, in the US, young people are often covered under their parents' insurance until age 26, or until an employer provides them with insurance. In the UK, health care is delivered via the National Health Service.

When choosing health care providers, consider:

- Location and accessibility
- Their experience and specialties
- Whether they accept your insurance
- Reviews and recommendations
- Available appointment times

Remember that telehealth (online appointments) is now an option for many services. While some situations require face-to-face visits, telehealth can be convenient for routine check-ups and quick consultations.

Understanding Insurance and Accessing Care

In some countries, accessing health care requires health insurance. Health insurance acts like a safety net — you pay a regular amount (called a premium) to avoid much bigger costs if you get sick or injured. While insurance terms can seem confusing at first, understanding the basics helps you make better decisions about your health care.

Your insurance policy will outline what's covered and what you need to pay. Usually, it will include:

- **Deductible:** An amount you pay before insurance kicks in. For example, with a $1,000 deductible, you pay the first $1,000 of health care costs. After that, your policy covers the rest. Typically, higher deductibles mean lower premiums.
- **Co-Pays:** Fixed fees for specific services. For example, a doctor's visit might cost you $20, and a prescription might cost you $10, with insurance covering the remainder.
- **Out-of-Pocket Costs**: Expenses not covered by insurance, including deductibles, co-pays, and costs that exceed your coverage or fall outside your policy's terms.

Accessing Affordable Care

Health care costs vary depending on where you live, but there are usually ways to get more affordable care. For example, students often have access to university health services. Community health centers and charitable clinics can also provide care at reduced costs. If you're worried about paying for health care, talk to your doctor or local health center about your options — there's usually help available.

Your Health, Your Life

Taking care of your health is key to staying fit and well throughout your life — and the earlier you start, the better. Building healthy habits now can prevent problems later and help you thrive in everything you do.

KEY TAKEAWAYS

- A healthy lifestyle combines good nutrition, sleep, exercise, and mental health.
- Prevention is easier than cure.
- Regular check-ups help catch issues early.
- Understanding basic health care helps you make good decisions.
- Taking care of your health is an investment in your future.

MOVING FORWARD

Nutrition plays a big role in maintaining a healthy lifestyle. The next chapter will dive into the details of nutrition, offering tips on getting the most out of your food and how to shop smart to get the best value for your money.

BUILDING HEALTHY EATING HABITS: FUELING YOUR BODY FOR SUCCESS

"One cannot think well, love well, sleep well, if one has not dined well."
— **Virginia Woolf**

Are you a "foodie," or do you eat just to survive? Either way, food is fundamental to your health. It provides the energy and nutrients your body needs to grow, repair, and function properly. Over time, a balanced and nutritious diet can help protect your health and well-being, empowering you to live a healthier and more vibrant life.

Before we begin, take a moment to reflect:

- How would you describe your current eating habits?
- What does "healthy eating" mean to you?
- What makes it hard to eat well?
- What small changes could you make today?

Healthy Eating: Your Foundation for Well-Being

A nutritious diet is key to overall health. Your body uses nutrients like building blocks, repairing itself and creating new cells. To keep your body functioning well, it's important to eat a variety of foods that supply all the necessary nutrients in the right amounts.

What Is a Balanced Diet?

You've probably heard the term "balanced diet," but there's often confusion about what it means. Despite all the hype around "superfoods" and trendy diets, a balanced diet is quite straightforward. It means eating a range of foods from different categories:

- **Healthy Fats:** Found in oily fish, nuts, seeds, and avocados
- **Proteins:** From meat, fish, eggs, beans, pulses, and tofu
- **Carbohydrates:** Including grains, pasta, bread, potatoes, and fruit

- **Vitamins and Minerals:** Found in all foods, especially vegetables
- **Dairy (or Dairy Alternatives)**: Found in milk, cheese, and yogurt

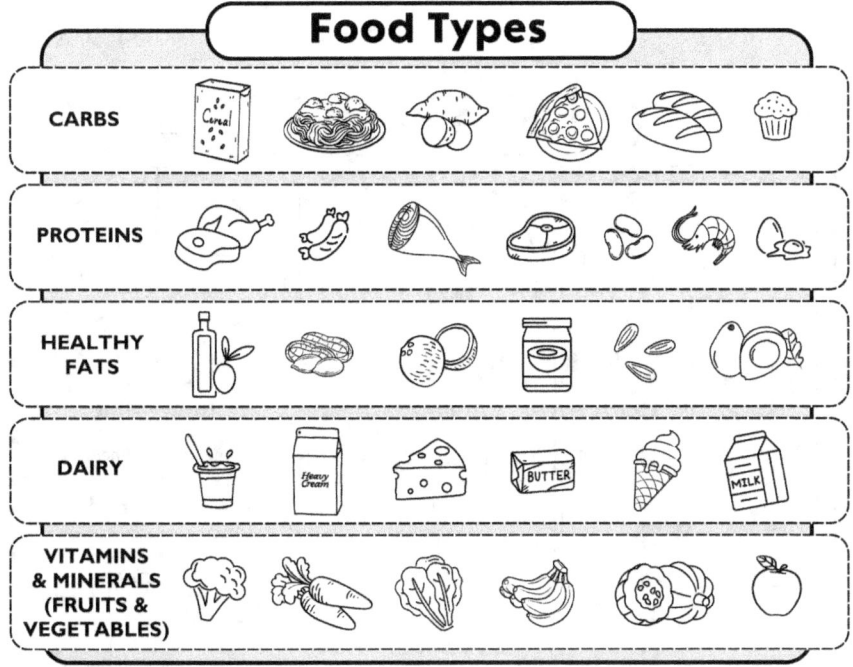

Your body needs a certain amount of each nutrient, but is flexible about where they come from. This is why a healthy diet can look different in different places around the world. For example, a balanced Japanese diet may look very different from a Greek one, but both can provide the same essential nutrients.

For each meal, try to include proteins, fats, and carbohydrates. A simple guideline is to fill half your plate with non-starchy vegetables, one-quarter with healthy carbs like brown rice, and one-quarter with protein. Healthy fats often come from the protein or the cooking method. Proteins and fats keep you full longer than carbs, so if you find yourself getting hungry soon after eating, try increasing your protein and healthy fat intake while reducing carbs.

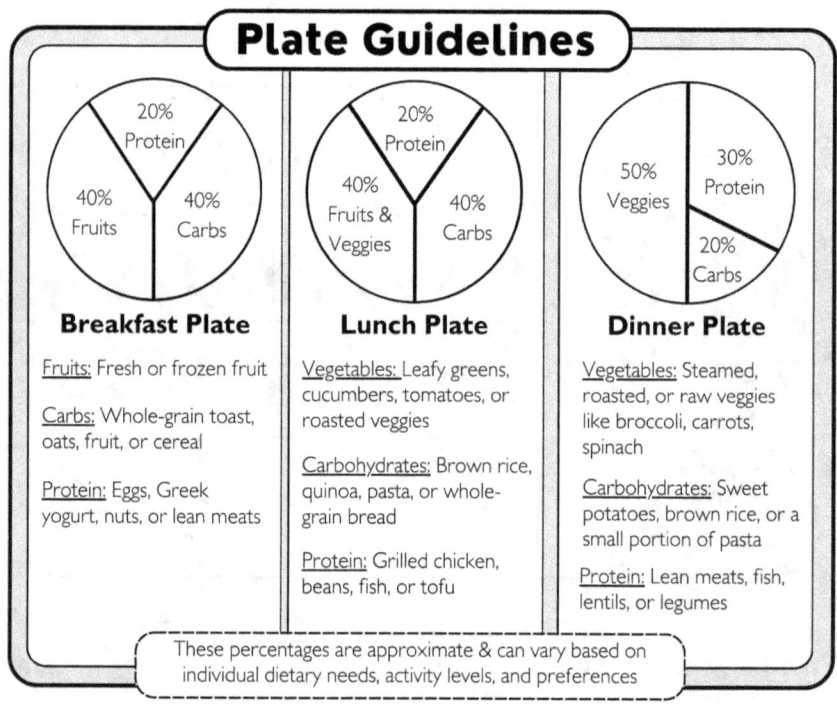

Food Facts

Look at your last meal:
- What colors were on your plate?
- Which food groups were included?
- What could you add to make it more balanced?

Try this with your next meal.

Reading Food Labels

Food labels provide essential information about what's in your food. While they might seem confusing at first, knowing how to read them helps you make better choices.

```
Nutrition Facts
Serving Size 1 cup (55g)
Servings Per Container about 12

Amount Per Serving        Cereal
Calories                     190
  Calories from Fat           10
                     % Daily Value
Total Fat 1g*
  Saturated Fat 0g            2%
  Trans Fat 0g                0%
Total Carbohydrate 45g
  Dietary Fiber 6g           24%
  Sugar 11g
Protein 5g
```

Ingredients List

Ingredients are listed by weight, from most to least. This means that if sugar is listed first, it's the main ingredient! Watch out for different names for sugar (like glucose, fructose, or anything ending in "-ose"), as they're all still sugar.

Nutrition Information

This table shows the amount of calories, protein, carbs, sugars, fats, and more. Values might be shown:

- Per serving (check the serving size!)
- Per 100g
- Per package

Mindful Eating: Understanding Your Body's Needs and Making Healthy Choices

Learning to listen to your body and understand its needs is a valuable skill. When unhealthy habits are ingrained, it can be hard to distinguish between what your body truly needs and what it craves.

Calories In, Calories Out

The energy you need daily varies by sex, age, height, weight, and activity level. Generally, most people need between 1,600 and 3,000 calories per day, with more active and larger individuals requiring more calories than those who are smaller and less active.

> **What Are Calories?**
>
> Calories measure the energy in food. Foods like fats are calorie-dense, while water-rich veggies like cucumbers have fewer calories. Your body uses these calories for everything it does, from breathing to running.

While calories are a common way to measure energy intake, they can be misleading, since everyone's body and needs are unique. Instead of obsessing over calorie counting, focus on eating a balanced diet and listening to your body's needs.

Budget-Friendly Kitchen Essentials: Tools, Storage, and Grocery Hacks

Cooking your own food is one of the easiest ways to improve your eating habits.

Preparing healthy, homemade meals can be both fun and rewarding, without being overly complicated. You don't need a fully stocked kitchen to get started, either. Start with the essentials, and build up your collection of tools over time.

Essential Kitchen Tools

Start with these basics:

- **Knives and Boards:** A good chef's knife and chopping board.
- **Cookware:** A frying pan and saucepan.
- **Utensils:** Wooden spoons, spatula, and measuring cups.
- **Storage:** Containers for leftovers.
- **Basic Appliances:** A small blender can be helpful.

> **Kitchen Confidence**
>
> I feel confident about:
> - Making breakfast   Yes | No
> - Following a recipe   Yes | No
> - Food safety   Yes | No
>
> Pick one "No" to work on this week.

COOKING AT HOME

Cooking for yourself gives you control over what goes into your food. It's also cheaper than eating out and a great way to learn a valuable life skill. You don't need to become a master chef — just learning how to prepare a few simple meals is a great start.

Cooking is also a fantastic way to connect with others. Whether you're making dinner with friends or family, sharing food brings people together. As you gain confidence in the kitchen, you might find yourself experimenting and enjoying the process even more.

Organizing Your Kitchen

A clutter-free kitchen makes cooking easier and more enjoyable. Try these tips:

- **Organize cupboards and drawers:** Arrange items by type and frequency of use. Keep frequently used goods at eye level and less-used items on higher or lower shelves.
- **Use clear containers and labels:** Label stored food with contents and dates for freshness tracking. Clear containers make it easy to see what's inside.
- **Maximize vertical space:** Add shelves, hooks, or hangers inside cupboard doors or on walls to store utensils, cookware, or smaller items.

Minimizing Waste

Wasting food is a drain on both your wallet and the environment. Keep waste to a minimum with these tips:

- **Plan your meals**: Before shopping, check what you already have and plan meals for the next few days or the week.
- **Avoid over-shopping**: Be realistic about what you'll eat, especially with perishable items. Stick to a shopping list to avoid impulse buys.
- **Use leftovers wisely**: Leftovers can make a great base for your next meal. Cool leftovers quickly and store them for later meals. They can be reheated as-is or repurposed into new dishes.

Budgeting for Groceries: Meal Planning and Shopping Strategies

Eating well doesn't have to break the bank — in fact, it can be incredibly rewarding to eat well on a budget! Here are some strategies to help you make the most of your grocery shopping:

- **Plan meals ahead:** Use ingredients you already have and plan meals to minimize waste. Simple dishes can often be the most satisfying.
- **Shop seasonally:** Seasonal produce is cheaper, tastier, and more environmentally friendly than out-of-season options.
- **Stick to your list:** A shopping list helps prevent unnecessary spending.
- **Avoid impulse buys:** If you are tempted by an unplanned item, wait until your next trip to see if you still want it.
- **Compare prices and look for deals:** Check prices at different stores and take advantage of sales and discounts.
- **Buy in bulk:** Staples like rice, pasta, and beans are often cheaper in bulk, provided you have the necessary storage space.
- **Opt for store brands:** Store-brand products usually offer similar quality at a lower price than name-brand options.

Eating Out and Delivery Services: Understanding Costs and Making Informed Choices

While cooking at home is nutritious, cost-effective, and satisfying, it's nice to treat yourself to a meal out or order in occasionally. However, doing so regularly can strain your wallet and is often less healthy, so consider it carefully before pressing "order!"

THE HIDDEN COSTS OF EATING OUT OR ORDERING IN

While eating out or getting takeout can be enjoyable, there are some hidden costs and downsides to consider:

- **Extra Charges:** Dining out or ordering in can be expensive. Beyond menu prices, factor in tips, service charges, delivery fees, and potential minimum order requirements that encourage overspending.
- **Large Portions:** Restaurants often serve large portions. To avoid overindulging, consider sharing a dish, saving leftovers, or asking for a to-go box.
- **Nutritional Unknowns:** When you're not the one cooking, it's hard to know exactly what's in your meal. Restaurant and takeout food often contains more salt, fat, and refined carbs than home-cooked meals.

Eat Well, Live Well

Taking charge of your nutrition is vital to leading a healthy, happy life. Food fuels your body, mind, and spirit, and learning the basics of nutrition and cooking is an investment in your well-being. By preparing your meals at home, you not only control what goes into your body, but also develop a rewarding skill that fosters creativity and connection.

Key Takeaways

- A balanced diet supports your overall health and well-being.
- Cooking at home saves money and gives you control over your meals.
- Staying organized in the kitchen reduces waste and simplifies meal prep.
- Food brings people together, building connections and memories.

Moving Forward

Good nutrition is just one part of a fulfilling life. Strong social connections also play a crucial role in well-being. The next chapter will explore building and maintaining meaningful relationships for a happier and more balanced future.

BUILDING YOUR SUPPORT SYSTEM: CULTIVATING STRONG AND HEALTHY RELATIONSHIPS

"Align yourself with the right people, forge the right relationships and you'll set yourself up for the long run."
—Daymond John

Relationships are the glue that holds life together. A strong support network makes navigating life's ups and downs easier, providing resilience, fresh perspectives, and a safe space to let off steam. And remember, it's a two-way street — being part of a strong network means supporting others just as they support you.

Before we begin, take a moment to reflect:

- Who makes up your support network right now?
- What makes a relationship healthy?
- How do you show support for others?
- What kind of relationships do you want to build?

Building and Maintaining Healthy Relationships

Your support system will be crucial throughout your life. Some people will stay in your network for years, while others will come and go. A strong support system usually includes a mix of different types of relationships:

- **Family**: Whether it's your birth family, chosen family, or extended relatives, families come in all shapes and sizes. They can provide security and unconditional love, but these relationships aren't always easy or perfect.
- **Friends**: Often called "the family we choose," good friends offer support, companionship, and a safe space to be yourself. It's essential to pick friends who are positive influences and make sure the friendships are healthy and balanced for everyone involved.
- **Partners**: Romantic partners offer emotional and physical intimacy, support, and shared life experiences. As with friends, it's important to choose a partner who aligns with your values and lifestyle, and to make sure the relationship is healthy.

- **Mentors**: Mentors provide valuable advice and guidance for personal and career growth. A good mentor can also connect you with other influential people, helping you expand your professional network.
- **Colleagues**: Even if you're not super close, work colleagues can offer strong support. They observe you in a professional setting and can provide career-related advice and encouragement.
- **Acquaintances**: People you see around or occasionally chat with but don't know well can still be important. They could become future friends or offer fresh perspectives and insights when you need them.

Together, these relationships create the social web that forms your support network, helping you navigate life's challenges and celebrations.

Connection Check

Think about today:
- Who made you smile?
- Who did you help?
- Who could you reach out to?

Make one connection plan for tomorrow.

THE STAGES OF A RELATIONSHIP

Most relationships go through several stages. Sometimes, these stages repeat as the relationship evolves:

- **Initial Formation**: This is the beginning phase, where you're getting to know each other and building trust. It's all about establishing a connection and seeing if you click.
- **Maintenance**: In this phase, you work to keep the relationship strong through mutual effort, open communication, and ongoing support. It's about nurturing the bond you've formed.
- **Challenges**: Every relationship faces bumps along the way. Whether it's disagreements or life changes, the key to overcoming these challenges is strong communication, adaptability, and resilience.
- **Growth or Ending**: Challenges often lead to growth and a stronger bond. But sometimes, they signal that it's time for the relationship to end. Ending a relationship doesn't mean it was a failure — it can be a natural and healthy part of life.

RELATIONSHIPS AND COMMUNICATION

Good communication is the foundation of any strong relationship. It's how people share their thoughts, feelings, and ideas, building stronger bonds and fostering empathy and respect.

Here are a few key principles for effective communication:

- **Active Listening**: Make a genuine effort to understand what the other person is saying and their perspective.
- **Setting Boundaries**: Clearly state what you're comfortable with in interactions, and establish your personal limits.
- **Being Assertive**: Communicate your thoughts and feelings directly and clearly, while being respectful of others.
- **Maintaining Trust and Respect**: Treat others fairly and avoid dishonesty or manipulative behavior.
- **Resolving Conflicts**: Address disagreements with respect, aim to find common ground, and be open to compromise.

Remember these principles when communicating in any relationship. While it can feel awkward or tough at first and you won't always get it right, good communication becomes easier with practice.

Communication Skills for Connection

If relationships are the glue that holds life together, communication is what makes that glue strong. Good communication skills help you connect meaningfully with others, work through problems, and handle conflicts with empathy.

THE IMPORTANCE OF ACTIVE LISTENING

Active listening means giving your full attention to the person speaking, and truly focusing on understanding their perspective. It reduces misunderstandings and helps build deeper connections through shared respect and empathy. Active listening boils down to three key points:

- Focus entirely on the speaker—both their words and body language.
- Try to understand their point of view, even if it's different from yours.
- Respond in a way that shows you've been listening.

> **Listen Up!**
>
> In your next conversation:
> - Count how many questions you ask.
> - Notice if you interrupt.
> - Watch the other person's expressions.
>
> What did you learn about your listening style?

Getting Your Point Across

Communication isn't just about listening — expressing your thoughts, opinions, and needs is just as important. While it can feel awkward sometimes, practice makes it easier. Try these tips to help others understand your perspective:

- Be direct and clear about what you mean.
- Use "I" statements to explain your perspective.
- Be confident while staying respectful of others' views.

Understanding Personal Boundaries

Personal boundaries are limits we establish in our interactions with others. While setting them can feel uncomfortable at first, they are essential for fostering mutual respect and protecting your emotional well-being.

Think of boundaries like the walls of your house — you decide who comes in and how close they get. Some boundaries might be:

- How much personal information you share
- How much time you spend with others
- What behavior you'll accept from others
- How you want to be treated

Your boundaries will vary depending on the relationship. What works for you might not work for someone else — and that's perfectly fine! The key is finding boundaries that suit your needs.

Here are some tips to help you set and maintain boundaries:

- **Know your limits**: Identify behaviors that make you feel stressed or uncomfortable. Consider setting boundaries around these areas. Remember that your feelings are valid and you deserve to feel safe and comfortable.
- **Communicate clearly**: Let people know what your boundaries are in a clear and specific way. Use "I" statements to express how you feel. For example, "I need 30 minutes to myself before bed" is more effective than "You never let me wind down before bed."
- **Stay consistent:** Stick to your boundaries and gently remind people, if needed. Let them know you appreciate when they respect your boundaries.
- **Respect others' boundaries**: Just as you want your boundaries respected, make sure to respect others' boundaries, too. Listen to what they tell you and understand that they deserve to feel comfortable and respected as much as you do.

Boundaries in Various Relationships

Your boundaries will vary depending on the relationship, and what works for you might not work for someone else — and that's perfectly fine. The key is finding boundaries that suit your needs.

Here are some examples of areas where boundaries might be set in different types of relationships:

- **Parents**: Privacy — like agreeing to knock before entering your room.
- **Siblings**: Personal space — agreeing not to invade your personal space or purposely annoy you.
- **Friends**: Support — setting boundaries around the level of emotional support you're comfortable providing or receiving.
- **Work**: Availability — establishing specific times when you're not expected to answer calls, emails, or messages.
- **Romantic Relationships**: All of the above. Romantic relationships cover many areas of life, making it essential to set clear boundaries around privacy, personal space, emotional and physical needs, and availability.

NAVIGATING CONFLICTS WITH EMPATHY AND RESPECT

Communication is rarely perfect, and misunderstandings are a normal part of life. Everyone can improve their communication skills, and even when you're a pro, disagreements will still arise.

Maintaining Respect During Disagreements

When disagreements happen, it's important to approach them with empathy, understanding, and respect. This helps prevent disagreements from escalating into conflicts, which are often more challenging to resolve. Here are some strategies to handle disagreements effectively:

- **Listen to understand**: Make an effort to understand the other person's perspective before presenting your own viewpoint.
- **Focus on the issue, not the person**: Address the problem itself, rather than attacking the person you're discussing it with. Aim for solutions, rather than assigning blame.
- **Stay calm:** Keep your emotions in check. Raising your voice can escalate the situation.
- **Be willing to find the middle ground:** Most disagreements require an element of compromise.

Sometimes the best solution is to agree to disagree and move on.

Solving Problems Together

The key to resolving problems and disagreements is working together to find a solution that works for everyone. Here's how:

- **Identify common goals**: Focus on what you both want to achieve, rather than your differences. When you find shared interests, solutions become clearer.
- **Explore options together:** Share ideas and listen to different views without judgment. Sometimes, the best solutions come from combining different perspectives.

- **Make an action plan:** Agree on specific steps forward. You might need to compromise, but finding a solution that works for everyone is worth it.
- **Follow through:** Do what you said you would. Check in with each other to make sure things are working. This builds trust for the future.

Finding Your Tribe: Family, Friends, Mentors, and Partners

"Call it a clan, call it a network, call it a tribe, call it a family: Whatever you call it, whoever you are, you need one."
— Jane Howard

Your "tribe" is made up of the people closest to you, whether they're friends, family, mentors, or partners. Each person brings something different to the table, and you probably bring something different to theirs. Over time, the people who make up your tribe might change — and that's completely normal. The key is to put in the effort to nurture those relationships, so everyone can support each other.

Communication, Respect, and Boundaries in Families

Communication is essential in any relationship — and family relationships are no different. But let's face it: Family dynamics can be tricky, and sometimes getting the message across isn't as easy as it sounds.

Easy or not, communication among family members is crucial for:

- Strengthening and maintaining bonds
- Expressing needs and emotions
- Resolving conflicts

Sometimes, family members can become so familiar with each other that they take each other for granted. Communication slips into unhealthy patterns, often without anyone meaning to disrespect one another. Whether you're a parent, step-parent, sibling, or child, everyone deserves respect, kindness, and space to be themselves.

You can't control how your family members behave, but you can control how you show up. If you notice unhealthy patterns, you can make a conscious effort to improve how you communicate. It's not about taking on all the responsibility or blame, but about working on yourself and helping prevent old habits from cropping up again.

Setting Boundaries

Even in families with good communication, setting boundaries is essential. Boundaries define what's acceptable and help preserve your personal space and emotional well-being. That can help prevent a lot of conflict down the road.

When Boundaries Aren't Enough

All families have their ups and downs, and open communication usually helps. But sometimes things go too far. If you ever feel in any kind of danger — physically or emotionally — you need to seek help from someone you trust, whether it's a teacher, health care provider, or another family member. Remember, you deserve to feel safe and respected.

FOSTERING MEANINGFUL FRIENDSHIPS

Friends are the members of your tribe that you probably have the most choice about. You choose whether to start, maintain, or end a friendship — something that's not always possible with family or mentors. The friendships that matter should be a source of support and positivity in your life.

The most important ingredient in a friendship is mutual respect and understanding. You don't need to be into the same things or come from the same background. In fact, some of the best friendships come from people who are totally different from you. If you stay open-minded, you'll find that you can make friends at any time, in any place.

Tips for Cultivating Friendships

Making friends can seem difficult and even scary, but with the right approach, it becomes much easier. Here are some tips to help you build meaningful friendships:

- **Be yourself**: Don't try to be someone you're not just to fit in. Authenticity attracts authenticity.
- **Show interest in others**: Be an active listener and genuinely care about what others have to say.
- **Look beyond the obvious**: Don't limit yourself to only talking to people who seem "like you." Sometimes, the best friendships come from unexpected places.
- **Get involved**: Join groups or activities that interest you. The more you participate, the more opportunities you'll have to connect with others.
- **Be reliable**: Follow through on your commitments. When you say you'll do something, do it. Trust is key in any friendship.

The Role of Mentors

Mentors are like a combination of colleagues, friends, and family. They're experienced people who provide guidance, advice, and support — especially when it comes to your career and personal growth. A good mentor can help you navigate the tough stuff, share valuable lessons, and connect you with other people who can help you along the way.

How to Find a Mentor

Here's how to find someone who can help you grow:

- **Clarify your goals**: Before looking for a mentor, figure out what you need from them. Are you looking for specific career advice, or do you want someone to guide you more generally? Do you need networking connections or help making a career shift?
- **Check your existing network**: Start by asking people you know for recommendations. Look for someone with relevant experience, strong communication skills, and a genuine interest in helping you.
- **Look beyond your circle**: Attend networking events, join professional organizations, or explore online networks. You never know when or where you might meet a potential mentor.
- **Approach respectfully**: Once you find someone who seems like a good fit, reach out and let them know you're interested. Be clear and respectful of their time, and don't be discouraged if they don't respond right away.

Healthy Communication and Respect in Romantic Relationships

Romantic relationships can be some of the most meaningful and significant connections we have. They should be a space where you feel supported and free to be yourself, but that only happens when there's good communication. Just like any other relationship, it all boils down to:

- Being honest and respectful
- Listening and responding appropriately
- Recognizing and respecting each other's perspectives
- Understanding and honoring boundaries

It's also important to have realistic expectations. Both you and your partner are individuals with lives outside of the relationship. Spending quality time together is important, but so is maintaining other relationships and giving each other space. A healthy balance is what keeps everything working.

Recognizing and Navigating Unhealthy Relationships: Setting Boundaries and Seeking Support

Not all relationships are healthy. While a good relationship can build you up, a toxic one can seriously hurt your confidence, mental health, and overall well-being. Some relationships might be unhealthy from the start, while others might develop that way over time. Either way, unhealthy relationships can take a major toll on you.

WARNING SIGNS OF UNHEALTHY RELATIONSHIPS

Unhealthy relationships rarely happen overnight. More often than not, there are early warning signs — red flags — that you shouldn't ignore. These behaviors can get worse over time, and sometimes lead to really dangerous situations. It's crucial to recognize these signs early, no matter what kind of relationship it is — family, friends, colleagues, or romantic partners.

Here are a few behaviors to look out for:

- **Disrespect**
  Disrespect might seem obvious at times, but it can be subtle, too. Over time, it chips away at your self-esteem, making it harder to speak up or even recognize when something's wrong. Examples include:
  - **Undue Criticism** — Belittling your feelings, ideas, or achievements
  - **Neglect** — Making you feel unimportant or disregarding your needs
  - **Deliberate Boundary Breaking** — Pushing past emotional, physical, or other boundaries

- **Emotional Manipulation**

  This can be tricky to recognize, but once it takes hold, it can make you question your own thoughts and feelings. Examples include:
  - **Gaslighting** — Twisting the truth to make you doubt your judgment
  - **Guilt-Tripping** — Making you feel bad about something you shouldn't feel guilty for
  - **Love-Bombing** — Overwhelming you with attention and affection to control you

- **Controlling Behavior**

  This can make you feel powerless and trapped. It often starts small, but can escalate. Examples include:
  - **Monitoring** — Wanting to know all the details about your activities
  - **Decision-making** — Telling you what to do, what to wear, or who to see
  - **Isolating** — Pressuring you to cut ties with friends, family, or anyone else

None of these behaviors will get better on their own. If someone is treating you this way, it's important to walk away — don't fall for the promise of change or apologies. If the behavior continues, it's time to protect yourself and prioritize your well-being.

SETTING BOUNDARIES AND PRIORITIZING SELF-RESPECT

Recognizing unhealthy behavior is one thing — setting boundaries and protecting yourself is another. It can be hard to see things clearly, especially when emotions are involved, but staying aware and acting on those feelings is crucial.

Establishing Boundaries in Romantic Relationships

Firm boundaries are your first line of defense. They let everyone know where you stand, and anyone who crosses those boundaries doesn't deserve your time. In a romantic relationship, setting boundaries involves:

- Knowing your limits
- Communicating them clearly
- Enforcing them consistently

Prioritizing Self-Respect

Your self-respect is a cornerstone of who you are. It affects how you show up in the world and how others treat you. If you start feeling like you're losing that respect, it's time to take action. It's tough to get back once it's gone, so don't let things slide.

To maintain your self-respect in a relationship:

- **Look after yourself** — Do things that make you feel good, both physically and mentally. Don't rely on your partner to take care of your well-being.
- **Remember that your needs matter** — Your feelings and needs are just as important as anyone else's. Don't let them slide in favor of your partner's.
- **Be prepared to walk away** — Sometimes relationships end. If they're not serving you, don't be afraid to leave.

SUPPORTING OTHERS IN UNHEALTHY RELATIONSHIPS

You can't always know what's going on in someone else's relationship, but if you notice signs of something unhealthy, it's okay to offer support. Signs include:

- Becoming withdrawn or subdued
- Unexplained change in personality
- Lashing out verbally or physically
- Behaving secretively
- Unexplained bruises or cuts

Offering Support, Safely

It can be tricky to know what to do if you suspect or know that someone is in an unhealthy relationship. They may not want to talk about it, and they may insist that nothing is wrong. Here are some ways in which you can help:

1. **Provide a safe space.** Let them know that you're there, no matter what.

2. **Respect their autonomy.** It's their decision, not yours, so don't try to force them to talk or make a choice.

3. **Don't confront the abuser.** Confronting the abuser could make things worse.

4. **Help with planning.** If they want to leave, support them with information about resources and safe options.

5. **Keep it confidential.** Don't share what's happening unless it's an immediate danger.

GETTING HELP

If you're experiencing abuse or violence in any of your relationships, you should seek help immediately. Talk to someone you trust and take steps to get out of the situation safely. You'll find resources locally or online that can help. Remember, no one deserves to stay in an abusive relationship.

Here are some places you can turn for support:

- **National Domestic Violence Hotline (US):** 1-800-799-7233 (SAFE), available 24/7
- **Women's Aid (UK):** https://www.womensaid.org.uk/
- **Respect (UK):** https://www.respect.org.uk/
- **Love is Respect (US):** https://www.loveisrespect.org/

- **Domestic Violence Resource Centre (Australia):** https://safeandequal.org.au/
- **Canadian Resource Centre for Victims of Crime (Canada):** https://crcvc.ca/

Supporting Your Future

The relationships you nurture now can stay with you throughout your life. By focusing on improving your communication skills, setting clear boundaries, and showing genuine respect and support for others, you can create strong, healthy connections. These relationships will form a reliable support network — an essential foundation for a happy, healthy, and successful life.

Key Takeaways

- Build a diverse support network of family, friends, and mentors.
- Communicate openly and address conflicts respectfully.
- Set and maintain clear boundaries in all relationships.
- Take care of yourself while supporting others.
- Remember that building strong relationships takes time and effort.

Moving Forward

The journey to independence and success is supported by the connections you build and maintain. Keep working on these skills, and you'll create a strong foundation for whatever comes next.

CONCLUSION

Congratulations! You've taken an important step toward building your future. By exploring this book, you've shown that you're ready to take charge of your life and create the future you want.

Think of the skills you've learned as tools in your life toolkit. You now have strategies to:

- Excel in your career
- Create your own space
- Make smart money choices
- Build strong relationships
- Take care of yourself
- Navigate the digital world

But this book is just the beginning. Your journey to independence will be unique to you, filled with opportunities to learn, grow, and discover who you are. You'll face challenges along the way — everyone does — but now you have the foundation to handle them with confidence.

Remember: Success isn't about getting everything right the first time. It's about being brave enough to try, resilient enough to bounce back, and smart enough to learn from every experience. You've already shown these qualities by preparing yourself for what's ahead.

Your future is waiting, and you're ready for it. Take that first step with confidence, knowing you have what it takes to create the life you want.

The journey begins now. Make it count!

THANKS
FOR READING MY
BOOK!

I truly hope you enjoyed the book and that the content is valuable now and in the future.

I would be grateful if you could leave an honest review or a star rating on Amazon.
(A star rating is just a couple of clicks away.)

By leaving a review, you'll help other parents discover this valuable resource for their children. Thank you!

To leave a review & help spread the word

www.ingramcontent.com/pod-product-compliance
Lightning Source LLC
Chambersburg PA
CBHW071206070526
44584CB00019B/2935